Chasing the Runner's High

My Sixty Million-Step Program

by

Ray Charbonneau

D1449693

First Printing

ISBN-13: 978-1-4538-4563-9
ISBN-10: 1-4538-4563-1

http://www.chasingtherunnershigh.com

TABLE OF CONTENTS

ACKNOWLEDGEMENTS

.... 5

AUTHOR'S NOTE

.... 7

CHAPTER 1

THE FIRST ONE'S FREE.. 9

CHAPTER 2

LIFE AS AN ADDICT 19

CHAPTER 3

STUFF – SHOES AND CLOTHES.. 43

CHAPTER 4

STUFF – GADGETS AND GEAR... 65

CHAPTER 5

INJURIES – WHEN DENIAL FAILS.. 79

CHAPTER 6

RACING IS A RUSH 95

CHAPTER 7

THE LONG ROAD TO THE MARATHON....................................... 117

CHAPTER 8

GOING FURTHER - ULTRAS 143

CHAPTER 9

GOING EVEN FURTHER 165

CHAPTER 10

MAYBE A LITTLE TOO FAR.. 193

CHAPTER 11

WHY KEEP RUNNING? 221

APPENDIX 1

ADVICE FOR THE NEW RUNNER 237

APPENDIX 2

EVEN MORE ADVICE 247

ABOUT THE AUTHOR

.... 261

Cover photo: Mile 95 of the 2004 Vermont 100 at 5:30AM
Sunday morning

Acknowledgements

Thanks to Ruth Sespaniak, Jim Chido, Mark Bates, Marie Charbonneau, and the Boston Writer's Meetup Group for their help with the creation of this book. Any errors that remain are all mine.

I'd like to thank everyone who's talked with me before, during, and after a run, helped put on a race, joined in on online discussions, or otherwise contributed to the community of runners that's helped shape my thoughts and encouraged me to keep going in spite of rain, mud, snow, and lazy Sunday mornings. I have received a lot of help from friends I've met and run with along the way. I hope I've paid a little of that back over the years by sharing stories and advice with less experienced runners. Hey, I've even written a book.

I'd like to dedicate this particular bit of sharing to:

- Dick Thomas, my manager when I started working at MIT, for showing me that even if you're not a champion, you can still run, have fun, and maybe enjoy a beer or two along the way.

- Steve Burton, the late coach of the Somerville Road Runners, who exemplified dedication to being the best runner he could be, and provided whatever help you needed to be as good as you wanted to be.

- Ruth Sespaniak, world-champion wife, who's love and support means more than I may ever be able to tell her, though I'll certainly keep trying.

Ray Charbonneau

Author's Note:

Thank you for reading <u>Chasing the Runner's High</u>. If you enjoy the book, please tell your friends about it! A portion of the profits from sales of "Chasing the Runner's High" will be donated to charity.

Additional copies of the book, in paper or in digital form for eBook readers, are available from:

http://www.chasingtherunnershigh.com

Ordering via my web site allows you to direct a portion of your purchase to the charity of your choice.

Digital editions are available in the standard ePub format, Adobe's PDF, and the .mobi format for the Kindle. All files are Digital Right Management-free. You can choose your own price for the eBook. See the web site for more information.

For centuries, public libraries have been providing books to everyone for free. Help keep that going. Library budgets are tight, so please consider buying a copy of <u>Chasing the Runner's High</u> for your local library. Order a copy, and have it sent to the library of your choice. If you do, I'd appreciate it if you sent a note to writeray@y42k.com so I can thank you for your generosity.

Running along Lake Champlain in the
2004 Green Mountain Marathon

Chapter 1: The First One's Free

"I have run most of my life on a small offshore Maine island where the main road is only 2 miles long. I estimate I have covered around 75,000 miles on that single piece of broken road. When you have absolutely no option of running a different or varied loop the only decision is whether you will run or not, and how far you will go. Running out on Great Cranberry Island made me feel at times like a caged lion and when I got out into the world to run a race it felt easy simply because I felt free."
                                        -Gary Allen

"Hi. My name is Ray and I'm an endorphin addict."

Most people, if they think about running at all, don't think much of the idea. They figure that running is for those scrawny, obsessive types. It's for the guys who don't eat meat, or would rather go out for a long run on Sunday instead of watching the game.

In truth, most runners are average guys or gals who've figured out that the enjoyment and benefits they get from running outweigh the risk of looking odd while running down a winter street in a reflective jacket and spandex tights. But there are some people who go past that and make running a central part of their lives. Some people even fixate on running to the extent that their relationship with the sport can start to look similar to an alcoholic's relationship with the bottle.

I'm one of those people. If I look at all the running I've done at one time or another, it looks a lot like addictive behavior. There's probably a free publication that describes people like me, available from the government print shop in Pueblo, Colorado:

- "Your family complains of your excess running." Been there.

- "Your running tolerance level has increased." It's called "getting in better shape."

- "You use running to cope with problems or to relax." Absolutely!

- "You sneak running alone." "Alone", yes. "Sneak"? Never! Well, hardly ever.

- "You are preoccupied with running." Check.

- "You rationalize your loss of control over running." Check – I'm doing it now.

- "Most of your friends or acquaintances are people you run with." Hmmm – my wife, most of my friends, my running club…Check.

- "You have lost days of school/work because of running." I've taken days off to go to a race. Check.

- "You have tried to quit running but cannot. (A good test is voluntarily going for six weeks without running and not experiencing physical or emotional distress.)" Voluntarily? The only time I stop is when an injury forces me to, and I usually start up again before I should. Check.

If you're familiar with 12 step treatment programs, you probably recognize the behavior pattern. And in spite of all this, I continue to justify my habit by telling myself that running is good for me.

Maybe it's just that 12 steps aren't enough? I track all my running in a log. The current version of my log is on my computer. One thing it does is automatically calculate the total number of miles I've run since I started logging everything back in 1992. I checked recently, and assuming that my stride length is approximately two feet, I figure that I've run just about 60 million steps. That represents a lot shoes. It also represents a lot of time; time to think, time to try out ideas, and time to form more than a few opinions about what and why.

In one of my early attempts at running when I was a little boy, I ran down some stairs, crashed into the sharp corner of a metal fireplace, and poked a hole in my head. I learned something valuable that day. I learned that I could get hurt running, but if I did, I could still get back on my feet and keep going. On the other hand, I didn't learn "Be careful when you run." That comes as no surprise to the people who know me.

George Sheehan, the runner and philosopher, once wrote that each runner is an experiment of one. I've continued to experiment since hitting the fireplace, and this book is my report of the results. Those results has been more successful than some, less successful than others. I've made plenty of mistakes, but that's how I learned. And that's part of what keeps running interesting. Every day there's something new to try, something that adds to the pile of facts, minutia, and trivia that I've accumulated.

I've learned a lot from other people too. Running is essentially a solitary pursuit. No one can run a step for you. But while you have to travel your own trail, part of what keeps it satisfying is the chance to cross paths with others who are following their own trails. When this happens, we get the opportunity to share ideas and encouragement. I've put some of what people have shared with me in these pages.

I spend a lot of time hanging out with other runners. Because of that, sometimes I forget that some of the things I've done that you'll read about in this book are unusual. I've accomplished some things as a runner that I'm proud of, but this book isn't about how great I am. I've never been the fastest or strongest runner and I'm OK with that.

I wouldn't say I'm a typical runner either. Actually, I'm not sure what a typical runner is. Is it a weekend jogger, or a sub-16 minute 5K racer, or someone who plans vacations so they can run a marathon in all 50 states, or a granola-eating, mountain-top-meditating, sure-footed trail runner? Whatever it is, I might be a little more determined or reckless than that. I've been known to push myself further, maybe too far sometimes.

How fast or far I can run isn't what's important. Over the years, I've tried a lot of things when I'm out on a run, or while I'm preparing for the next run. I've learned (and relearned) quite a few things about running and about myself while performing my own ongoing experiment. That's what's important.

There are plenty of tips in this book, but it's not a "how to run" guide. I'm going to tell you what I've done before and what I do now, but I don't believe I have all the answers. I'm always looking for new ideas to try and incorporating the ones that seem to be helpful.

What works for me may not work or may be less important for you. You're a different person, with different strengths and weaknesses. This book is just more input for your own experiment of one. In the end, you have to decide for yourself what's best. No one can run for you.

Whether you run 10 miles in a week for exercise or 100 miles in a day for a race, you'll probably be able to identify with many of my experiences. If I can explain to myself why I spend so much time, often while fighting through pain, on a somewhat selfish, solitary activity, then maybe you'll get something out of that explanation too.

If you're in a relationship with someone who doesn't run or you have friends who question why you spend so much time running, give them a copy of this book. With any luck it will help make it easier for these people to understand why their running friend heads out the door even when it's 40°, windy, and raining outside. And why that runner needs to spend half an hour deciding what to wear before they go out.

Everybody's seen a TV show or a movie where a drug dealer tells his customer "The first one's free." Some addictions are that powerful, powerful enough that all it takes is one dose to get started. Maybe it's a chemical reaction, maybe the feeling just fills a need that you didn't even know you had. You might not be obsessed yet, but you've found something you will try again, even if you have to pay.

My first drinks were from a bottle my parents had stored in a closet. When I felt the effect, I knew I had found something I liked. I didn't have to earn the right to keep drinking. It wasn't hard to fill another glass. When I was old enough, all it took was money.

Running isn't quite like that. There's a reason runners say "My sport is your sport's punishment." It's hard work. If you're considering running, let me warn you - suffering is not optional. You will get tired and sweaty and sore. You'll be out in broiling summer heat and damp, icy, and windy winter cold. You'll develop nagging injuries. That's how you pay for your fun.

It's easy to give running a try, but a running addiction takes some time to develop. It takes an effort to build the endurance that makes running easy enough to be fun and relaxing. Not everyone feels that the rewards of running outweigh the discomforts. A lot of people drop out before they're fit enough to run as far as is necessary to get the endorphins to kick in, or they just don't get hooked on the experience and move on to another activity. Other people grit their teeth and keep a minimal running schedule just for fitness sake. Many people drink, but not everyone goes on to become an alcoholic.

Ask any runner, and they'll have their own reason for how they got started on the path. If you're destined to be a runner, all it takes is one. Vanity was the main reason I started running. I ran to keep my weight down, and it worked. As I ran, I found other reasons to keep it up. I took to running and never looked back

Running keeps me thin, and it also helps develop muscle tone which makes my legs and butt look more appealing. That's a good thing, because runners spend a lot of time in shorts or spandex tights. My wife tells me I don't look too bad in those spandex tights, for a guy (as long as I don't pick an exceptionally colorful pair).

Starting the day with a run works better than coffee to wake me up and get me going. An evening run gives me something to look forward to after a long day at work.

Running helps me balance out days spent behind a desk, or nights spent at my favorite bar. As it happens, one mile of running burns off about one beer's worth of calories. I run a mile in less than 10 minutes, even at my slowest, so unless I'm pounding down the beers pretty fast, running takes off weight faster than beer puts it on.

The fitness I get from running gives me more vigor for my day-to-day activities. I have the energy for whatever it is I'm doing that day, whether it's dreary, like housecleaning, or something more fun. Because I run, I can join in with my friends when they're doing their favorite outdoor activities. Running takes up a lot of my time, but when I go out for a bike ride, go skiing, go on a hike, or play basketball, I'm usually fit enough to keep up.

Can you think of other activities that are more pleasurable with a little extra endurance? I can, and so can your significant other.

I wasn't always patient enough with myself when I got started. Addicts are greedy. I was having a lot of fun with my new toy, and I wanted to do everything -- run faster in shorter races, run marathons, and even qualify to run the Boston Marathon. And I wanted it *now*. I added mileage to my weekly routine too quickly, did too much hard running, and didn't allow enough recovery time. I had foot problems, knee problems, and spent a lot of time battling colds and other minor illnesses.

I was brought up with a well-developed sense of responsibility (and guilt), so the natural thing for me to do when I didn't get the results I wanted was to work harder. But I was already working too hard, or working hard the wrong way, and doing even more of the same obviously wasn't going to help. Slowly, I began to figure out the things that were working for me. Even more importantly, I started to figure out the things that weren't working. It's an ongoing process, but I use what I learn to adjust my running routine, making changes as my ability improves or I learn a new trick.

The effort has paid off. I like being fit enough to know that if necessary I can run the 10 miles home after a late night show. I like being fit enough to go out for a long bike ride or a few hours in a kayak even though I never train for those activities. I like competing against myself to see how fast or how far I can go, and I like competing against other people in races. I like runners and having running to keep us occupied when we get together. I like eating whatever I want. I like going for an early morning jog with my wife before we split up for the day. I like the meditative state I can get into through the repetitive act of running that often appears in the middle third of a run, after I've warmed up but before I start to get tired. I like finding loose change or a lost toy by the side of the road. I like the way I can use running to burn off adrenaline while I think through frustrations that crop up in other parts of my life. I like running in the city, where there's a lot to look at as I run by. I like running in the country or the woods, where it's quiet, there's nice scenery, and the air is fresh. I like finishing a run and knowing that once again, I've put in my time and kept my commitment to myself. I like knowing that if I can run for hours in the heat or cold or wind or rain, I can certainly sit through an hour long meeting at work. Most of all I like a nice comfortable 5-mile run, the kind that's made possible by lots of hard 10-mile runs.

There's a lot of repetition in running. When you're taking millions of steps, a lot of them are going to be very similar. But there's comfort in that too, comfort in knowing that if I just keep running, I'm sure to make it to the finish, because I always have before.

This blurry photo from a 1978 meet in Hinesburg, VT is the only remaining evidence of my high school track career

Chapter 2: Life as an Addict

"I started running in 6th grade. Why? To see if I could beat the bus home at lunchtime. I lived less than a mile from school, 11 blocks to be exact, so I was ineligible to take the school bus to and fro for lunch. The second the lunch bell rang, I was out the door like a flash, tearing down Larchmont Avenue to the Sound like nobody's business. Some days it was close and I beat the bus by maybe a nose, but most days I beat that sucka clean!"
-Jim Chido

As far as I know, I am the first running addict in my family. Some people think addictions are hereditary, but neither my parents nor my siblings run. In my extended family, I have an uncle who used to run, but he gave it up and has never looked back. I also have a cousin who was a race director for a few years, but she did that to support her town. She didn't run herself.

It all started when I was a little kid. Like most people, the first thing I did after I learned to walk was give running a try. Once I stopped falling and bumping into things, I was buzzing around the house and yard, exploring my newly expanded world. Running came naturally, along with eating, sleeping, and learning from my parents.

I was a quiet kid. I liked to spend a lot of time by myself reading, but I also liked to get out and do things and be with people. I didn't always fit in easily with the others, but the games we played gave us something in common to do or to talk about.

My friends and I all ran while we were growing up in Vermont. We had so much energy that it burst out almost by itself. We played games like Tag or Kill the Guy with the Ball that were basically just excuses to sprint around the neighborhood. We ran (and biked) from place to place, because we were in a hurry to get to the next thing, and because we could.

As we got older, the games got more organized. I played whatever sport was in season, whenever we had time and could get a group together. I played a lot of baseball, basketball, football, bowling, and frisbee, and dabbled in a variety of other activities.

Sports were also a way to get my dad's attention. My dad played baseball and other sports when he was growing up, and competed for his school when he was old enough. After he got a job and started a family, he still got out and played softball with the guys at the office. As he got older, his social life revolved around more sedate ways to compete, like golf and bowling (and bridge). Dad encouraged his sons to play sports, coaching our Little League teams and going to our other events when work permitted.

But as time passed, I was forced to spend more time sitting down. First, I started spending eight hours a day in school, where all the running around was concentrated into relatively short periods during gym class, recess, and maybe lunch. Then I advanced to high school, where they took recess away from us.

High school track was where I first started running as a specific, organized activity, rather than just as play. I wasn't motivated by fitness or weight loss or any of those health-related things. I started running track partly for the thrill of competition, and partly to belong.

I wanted to play, not just sit there and watch the cool kids compete. I was good at schoolwork, but that's never been a ticket to higher social status in the cutthroat world of teenagers.

Track wasn't my first choice. Unfortunately, I didn't hit very well, I had no jump shot, I never learned to skate backwards, and I wasn't big enough for football. The closest I got to playing one of the major team sports was when I tried out for the baseball team as a freshman. After I got cut, I volunteered to be the scorekeeper.

In my sophomore year, I considered track as a possibility. When we had races in gym class, I was faster than most people. And nobody got cut from the track team. Being on the track team didn't automatically make me a popular person at school, but it was better than nothing.

The football coaching staff had spare time in the spring, so they coached the track team. Our coaches were mostly concerned with keeping the football players fit for the fall. The rest of us were on our own as far as training was concerned. As spring approached, we showed up after school, did pretty much whatever we wanted to at practice, and went home. When school let out for the summer, we put training aside. I don't think anybody trained over the weekend, let alone year-round.

Vermont's lengthy winters meant the spring track season wasn't very long. To get a head start, we held some practices indoors before the snow on the track melted. Runners had two options. We could do short sprints in the hallway, and try desperately to stop before we crashed into the wall. Or we could run the stairs. The stairs were probably better for us, but they were nowhere near as much fun.

When the snow finally melted, we headed outdoors to the track. At practice, the coaches usually left us to run our events multiple times. I guess they figured that if we did the same thing over and over again, we'd get better at it, so around the track we went. Sometimes we had to dodge baseball players while we ran as they shuffled through a lap or two as part of their practice.

I ran the 220, 440, the mile relay, and I high-jumped. I had fun, but without a real training plan, I never reached my potential. That's too bad, because I was young, and I still had the flexibility and resiliency to tolerate the stress of sprinting. High school would have been the best time for me to try running all-out for pure speed. I still have my high school track spikes today, but just looking at them makes my feet hurt.

When I graduated from high school, I stopped running. I went to college, but I didn't go out for the track team or the cross-country team. I had some mild regret that I wasn't as fit as I was in high school, so I did a little running, but not in any organized fashion. I was old enough to drink now, and that path to overcoming social awkwardness required much less effort. And before long I dropped out of college, started working, and stopped running altogether.

A lot of my early jobs involved standing in place, either behind the counter at a store, or in uniform, guarding something that didn't really need guarding. After a while, I moved up to office jobs, where I just sat there on my butt for lengthy parts of the day. When I left the office, I'd eat, go out for drinks, or sit in front of the TV and click the remote.

In my early 30's, I was working at MIT, getting fatter, and looking for something to do. I played softball, which was in large part an excuse to hang out with people and drink beer, and I played in a weekly roller hockey game with some of the students, but I wanted more.

My boss at MIT was Dick Thomas. He was an older guy who also liked his beer. He wasn't some super-fanatical fitness freak, but Dick had run the Boston Marathon a couple of times, getting his number through a connection since he wasn't fast enough to run the required qualifying time. Talking about Dick's running got me thinking about running again, and helped me realize that running could be fun, even if I wasn't the fastest guy out there. I started to regret that I wasn't running anymore.

One spring I even tried to run a little bit. I bought a pair of Nike Air Pegasus shoes, and every couple of days I went out and ran around the block until I got tired, which took me less than a mile. But that didn't last for long. The air pod in one of my shoes went flat, softball season came along, and I quit running again.

When I was 31, I weighed 165 pounds, almost 40 pounds heavier than I was in high school. I hadn't gotten any taller (I'm 5'8"), so I carried most of the weight in a potbelly. Since I was a short person with a small frame, the potbelly made me feel a little ridiculous. For a while, I was in denial about it. I told myself I was reasonably active. I played softball, I biked some, I could keep up with the younger students at roller hockey, and I was fit enough to do other things once in a while when an opportunity presented itself. I'd loosen my belt, leave my pants unbuttoned, and leave my shirt untucked to cover it all.

After a year or two of that, I finally decided it was time to do something about my weight. I cut back on the amount I ate and I bought an exercise bike. For weeks, I ate a meal substitute drink and rice cakes for breakfast and lunch. I set the bike up in my apartment kitchen and I rode it for 15 minutes every afternoon after I got home from work. After I finished riding, I had a small meal for dinner, with the bike there in the kitchen as a reminder to keep me from cheating.

This program was no fun at all, but it worked. After a couple of months, I got my weight back under 140 pounds. But I was hungry all the time, and riding the bike was mind-numbingly boring. I wasn't going to be able to keep my weight down unless I found something that I enjoyed more than living like a gerbil, eating cardboard and spinning a wheel in a cage.

I wanted something I could do by myself so I wouldn't have to depend on other people. I wanted something I could easily fit into my schedule. I didn't want to buy a lot of expensive equipment, in case I didn't stick with it. I wanted something that I could do outdoors, anywhere I was, but certainly away from the confines of my office and my apartment. And of course, I wanted the exercise to be intense enough so I could eat regularly again and still keep my weight down without spending my whole life exercising. There was only one thing that I could think of that met all of those needs – running.

At first, I ran from my apartment to a large field at nearby Tufts University. A loop around that field was about a half-mile (or so I told myself). I ran around and around the edge of the field until I got tired, and then I ran home. Running on grass was easier on my feet and legs while I built up strength, and I enjoyed it more than running on sidewalks.

My addiction crept up on me. I never made a conscious decision to keep running. After a while, I just began to take it for granted that running was part of my future plans. I started rearranging other activities so they didn't interfere with my running schedule. When I got bored with the endless loops in the field, I started to trace out running routes of different lengths on the streets in my neighborhood. I started looking for ways to run farther or faster, and started thinking about goals. Soon I was entering races and dreaming of running Boston myself.

As an addict, I'm always thinking about my next run. I used to worry more about my speed, but once I looked at it objectively, there was no practical purpose in trying to squeeze out every last bit of my potential as a runner. I've proved that no matter how hard I work, I'm not going to be an Olympic champion. I'm still working on accepting that. Maybe in a few more years. In the meantime, I plan each run starting with the basic rule that if it's not fun, I'm working too hard. Running isn't just about fitness.

Each day's plan starts with deciding where I'm going to run. I live in Arlington, Massachusetts, a suburban town northwest of Boston. I know the streets in Arlington better than anyone who depends on their car for transportation. From Arlington, I have a multitude of running routes to choose from. The farther I'm going to run, the more choices I have. Every one of these choices can lead to a new adventure. But even if I've run a route hundreds of times, there's still the chance that this time I'll see something I've never seen before. And though I've already run many different courses, there are still plenty of new places to go.

I usually just go out my front door and start running, unless I'm meeting up with someone else. Some people like to drive to a park or some other nice area and run there. I'm glad I don't have to drive to run. It seems counterproductive.

From my front door, I can run through quiet suburbs, passing through the compact groups of shops that interrupt the residential areas. If I get up early enough, I can sometimes see rabbits along the bike path that runs through the fields near the public transit station. For some reason, seeing wild bunnies is usually a portent of a good day.

I can run on calm side streets or wide main roads. Quiet roads let me focus on running or my thoughts, with less worrying about traffic. Busy roads are usually more direct routes to new places, and they're useful in the winter when they're plowed and clear while less active roads are narrow and still snow-covered.

I can run through the more hectic suburbs to my south, right into downtown Boston. Or I can take a less direct route, and loop into Boston from the west so I can pick up the Boston Marathon course and run through the Newton hills into town. When I reach the city, there are more people and buildings to distract and amuse me as I run by, and sidewalks to run on if the traffic is too heavy. I become part of the bustle, weaving my way through all the activity on the streets or along the waterfront. There are plenty of stores where I can buy things I might need, or bathrooms with sinks for refilling bottles and toilets for the usual needs.

I'm a distance measurer. I like to track how far I run each day and watch the numbers mount in my log. Some people approximate how far they run by using the time they spend running and an estimate of their pace, but that's not accurate enough for me. Actually, I don't bother to time most of my training runs. If I did time myself, I'd be tempted to turn every run into a race and try to go faster than before, especially if I was running one of my regular routes. Logically, I know that no one can run faster every time they go out, but I'm not always logical. Whenever the watch showed that I didn't run fast, I'd inevitably be at least a little disappointed, and who needs that?

Where I live, no matter what distance I choose to run, I can put together a flat route or mix in a wide variety of hills. It's harder to find flat routes – roads that are flat when I'm in a car grow hills when I'm traveling on foot. If I want a real change, I can go to the Middlesex Fells Reservation, where there are miles of wooded trails, ranging from easy fire roads to rocky, hilly single-track.

Since I usually run from my house, I usually run courses that I've run before. I have one or more pre-planned routes for every distance up to about 20 miles. When I'm re-running a favorite route, there's no need to worry about where I'm going or how much farther I have to run. The fewer choices I have to make, the more I can relax and live in the moment, and enjoy running for itself. When I have to keep deciding where I'm going to run next, the temptation to turn towards home is always there. No matter how much I like to run, part of me is always ready to bask in the comfort of finishing, so if I don't have to think about whether it's time to go home, I'm happier.

I have one 12-mile loop that I've been using for years, almost as long as I've been able to run that far. I've moved four times since I began using the loop. After each move I was able to continue using the loop from the new house with only minor modifications, even though that never was a priority when choosing my new home. Most of my shorter runs use segments of this loop, which mixes together flat and hilly sections on urban streets and lakeside parkways. They're all roads that are wide enough to run when there's traffic, and roads where the plows and cars clear the snow quickly. The biggest danger running this loop is that I've run it so often, I can run it without paying much attention. Sometimes I get lost in my head and don't watch for cars as much as I should. That never lasts long, as the drivers are happy to use their horns to get me to wake up.

When I'm paying attention, I always stop for cars before I cross the street. When cars stop and wave me across, it's nice, but I have to stop anyhow, since I can never be sure what the car is going to do. It's quicker and wastes less gas if they just go, and I can always use the rest. I never jog in place when I'm stopped at a corner. A 7-minute mile with a one minute rest at the corner is still an 8-minute mile, and jogging in place just looks silly.

Sometimes it's fun to get away from my regular routes, especially if I'm going on a long run. I'll take my GPS (gotta keep track of the distance!) and head out without a planned route. I can often fool myself into running longer this way.

One way I trick myself is to decide to run a certain number of miles, go more or less straight out for half of that distance, then come back home by a different route. Since the out leg is straight, any different route that I take back has to be longer. I'm not really fooling myself, but I always get a little satisfaction out of running farther than I "planned".

If the run is going to be long enough, I'll bring my transit pass in case I need a ride back. I haven't <u>had</u> to use it yet, but you never know. If I'm going over 15 miles, I'll add some energy gel packets to help keep me going, both physically and mentally. The easily digestible carbohydrates in a gel provide a quick lift, but once I take one, I have to keep taking them to avoid a crash once the sugar runs out. I find that if I take one every 5 or 6 miles, that's often enough.

When I cross paths with other runners, most of the time we just acknowledge each other with a wave or nod and continue on. Sometimes I'll come up on someone running in my direction at a similar pace, and we'll run together for a while, usually sharing running stories.

It always surprises me how many people ignore other runners totally. Maybe they're afraid of strangers or embarrassed by their lack of speed or the way they look in tights, but they just keep their heads down and their iPods turned up, and they don't act like they're part of a community. That's their loss.

Running does attract a greater proportion of loners than other sports. Running meshes well with an introverted lifestyle. The nature of the sport means that most runners spend a lot of time alone. Even if you choose to do a lot of running with other people, no one can run for you. Running can give an introvert the comforting feeling that he controls his own destiny, instead of being subject to the inexplicable whims of other people. And running provides a social framework where an introvert can easily meet people with whom he has something in common. That gives the people who need it a way to break the ice.

I've been running for years, and there are still days where it's an effort for me to get myself organized and out the door for my run. It happens to everybody, even running addicts. On the days when it's tough to get going, I do whatever I can to distract myself and avoid thinking while I put on my running shoes and get myself out the door to slog through the run. Afterwards, I always feel good because I didn't give in. I'm also happy that I had a good run, or if the run itself wasn't great, I'm happy that I got it over with. By running on the days I don't feel like running, I stay in shape so I can run on the days I do.

When I get tired of choosing my own course, I can get together with friends from my running club, the Somerville Road Runners. SRR has grown from the group of 30 or so of us that started the club to over 400 runners.

Running is often a solitary pursuit, but it changes into a social activity when I'm running with my club. There are all kinds of people in the club. Runners aren't saints. Some runners look down on slower runners and revel in their own successes at the expense of others. The guy who stabs people in the back at work isn't going to be different when he's running. Other runners may not be jerks, but might have issues with socializing, self-esteem, or substance abuse. Running isn't some magic cure-all. If a runner has a problem, he takes it with him when he laces on his running shoes.

But most people are friendly once you get to know them. There are plenty of outgoing, jovial runners who see running as a way to work off a few excess pounds while they hang out with their friends. Other people love to organize events, and find an outlet in managing clubs and races. There are people who like helping, and running provides plenty of opportunities for them to volunteer. They do their best to help everyone accomplish their goals, and they celebrate other people's victories, large and small.

I'm always ready to go running with my friends. Running with other people helps make running more enjoyable, and you can help keep each other motivated. If nothing else, running with other people helps pass the time.

We get together outside of running too. For example, Dan Solomon, former club president, is a good friend who was both my divorce lawyer and the Justice of the Peace at my second wedding. Ruth enjoys telling her friends that one of our early dates was when we went to my divorce lawyer's wedding.

The club has track workouts on Tuesday nights. A track workout is a great way to run precise workouts geared to your particular needs and goals. On the other hand, running in small, flat circles on a track can get tedious. Ruth went to the Tuesday workouts when she started running and that helped her in her races, but I find that I get hurt more often when I go to the track for my speed workouts.

Instead, I usually use the club's weekly Thursday night pub run for my version of speedwork. It's a free timed fun run that we've been doing every Thursday in Somerville since 1995, regardless of rain, snow, traffic, Thanksgiving, a fire that closed the bar down for a year, or other impediments. The run actually pre-dates the formation of SRR. A group of us were showing up regularly on Thursdays and we decided that we might as well get organized and start a club.

The run is open to all, not just club members, and we advertise it on running calendars, so we get a variety of people showing up. We get people out for a fun run, regulars looking to hang out with their friends and maybe improve their time, and out-of-towners looking for someone to run with. We've even had a Kenyan earning his living in this country from road race prize money show up for a couple of between-race workouts.

For years, we'd gather every week at Khoury's, a local dive bar, troop outside to the fire hydrant by the front door and listen to any pre-run announcements with Winter Hill looming over us in the distance. Then we'd take off on the 4.13-mile loop. The first mile of the course climbs up the hill at a steep 5% grade, and then it rolls on from there, finally flattening out for the last mile or so. At the finish, you'd get your time, cool down, and hang out outside for a while, talking and cheering in other runners, until it was time to go back in the bar for more talk and perhaps a beer or three.

Khoury's always had a sleazy reputation, and recently the city closed them down. We've moved the pre-and post-race activities down the street to Casey's, another local bar, and continued the run every Thursday without missing a beat. The move to a nicer bar and the addition of free post-run pizza has helped bring in a new group of people, and the tradition is hopefully set to survive for another 14 years.

Over the years, we've added other weekly events to the Thursday night run. Tuesday night track practice came first. Then in 2009, the club started another weekly run from a bar in Davis Square in Somerville on Mondays. This run is 3 miles, and hosted by The Burren, a bar that's even nicer than Casey's. The Burren provides free Guinness beef stew and vegetarian pasta for the runners.

The Burren is only two miles from home, so I often warm up by running there and and cool down by running back. Casey's is four miles away. I can run there and back, but sometimes I'll run there, run the course, and then ride home with Ruth. That way I can spend more time hanging out afterwards, eat some pizza, and avoid running home with a full stomach.

Another benefit of belonging to the club is that it makes it easier to find companions for my long, slow training runs. I love to run by myself, but I also love to go out with a group and let the conversation and the momentum of the pack carry me along.

SRR doesn't have regular "official" long runs at the same time and place every week like some clubs do. Instead, especially during the spring and fall marathon seasons, someone will volunteer to host a run and share some of their favorite running routes. Anyone who's interested meets at the home of the host, and then people split up into groups according to their distance goals for the day and head out, dividing up further by pace as the run proceeds. The runners trickle back in after they're done and sit and rest for a while, greeting the rest of the group as they arrive and refueling from the spread of healthy and not-so-healthy food provided by the host. If Ruth and I are hosting a run, she'll make some delicious home-baked goodie, while I'll whip up a batch of fruit smoothies, my ideal refueling comfort food.

Other times groups of friends get together informally to put in their miles. We'll meet at a home or at a local landmark, maybe a transit station, and head off. Sometimes we'll stop in a coffee shop afterwards to recover with a pastry or two, or sometimes individuals peel off from the group one-by-one once they've run enough, until the remaining few decide to pack it in and head for home.

SRR puts on four "real" races, with registration fees, numbers, t-shirts, and the works, along with the runs from Casey's and The Burren. A ton of work goes into putting on any decent race, no matter how small. Luckily, there are people who willingly take on the responsibility and build all the events that fill the yearly race calendar.

The An Ras Mor is a flat, fast 5K in Cambridge in March. It's a St. Patrick's Day race, hosted by an Irish pub. We provide free beer and food outdoors afterwards. Sometimes we don't need coolers to keep the beer cold, but everyone still has fun.

The Summer Steamer is our oldest race. The first one was held in 1991, before the club was organized. It's run on the Khoury's Thursday night course, only this time it's an official race, so runners get a chance to see how fast they can go when they don't have to watch out for cars. It's a small race with free beer and food (notice a theme?). The numbers get a boost every few years when the race is part of the New England Runner's Pub Series or the Hocomock Swamp Rat Grand Pricks series.

The 24 Hour Around the Lake is an ultramarathon run on a 5K loop around a lake in Wakefield. It starts at 7PM on a Friday and continues, often in brutal summer heat, until 7PM on Saturday. You can choose from four events. Three of the events start Friday night at 7PM: the 24-hour ultra, a 12-hour overnight ultra, and a flat, fast marathon. There's also a 12-hour ultra that starts at 7AM Saturday for those that prefer sleeping at night or running in the sun. It's a challenging event for tough people who are strong enough keep running and ignore the tantalizing call of the cool waters of the hotel pool when they pass it by at the end of every loop.

Our largest race is the Gobble Gobble Gobble. The race has grown each year, and now there are well over 2000 runners showing up to run the 4 mile course on Thanksgiving morning. The Burren provides space for the usual free beer afterwards, but sadly, only a limited few can crowd inside. Everyone else heads home with their hunger sharpened for the big feast.

Unless we're out of town, Ruth and I always volunteer to help out at SRR's races. We figure working races four times a year instead of running is the least we can to do to give something back to the community. The races also make enough money so the club has been able to donate more than $100,000 to area charities.

If there's going to be a club to put on races, someone has to manage the club. Club administration can be a thankless job. A core group of people make the decisions and carry out the tasks that are necessary to keep things running. I used to go to most of the meetings, and I was the club's first webmaster, but I did my time when the club was smaller and the jobs were easier.

Plenty of other volunteer opportunities exist. The club has sent people to help with area cleanup opportunities, collected money for charity efforts, and provided support for races put on by other organizations. I hooked up with another running club through SRR, the group at the Medford Boys & Girls Club. Weekly, when the weather allows it, I help the club staff take any of the kids who are interested out for a run. We might herd them along the streets for a couple miles or take them to a nearby park for relays, freeze tag, and other games.

There are many other activities to keep everyone busy. The club charters a bus to the start of the Boston Marathon, and has arranged group travel to other races or for fun events like ski trips or hikes. The club has a holiday party every year where we present awards for things like "Most Improved Runner" or to members who attend all of the races chosen as the SRR "Race of the Month" or who represent the club in all of the USATF Grand Prix races. Club members have formed "The IT Band" (named after the leg's oft-injured illiotibial band) to play music at the holiday party and at charity fundraising events. I've run through the streets of Somerville at Christmastime wrapped in battery-powered flashing LEDs as part of a group of runners and customized bike riders visiting the best home lighting displays.

There are special events at some of the weekly Thursday runs. The yearly "Birthday Run" marks the anniversary of the club, and a prize is presented to the runner who comes closest to running the course in his or her birthday suit, a special challenge in New England in February. Lately we've been adding to the post-run feed with cooking contests. Contestants compete to see who can make the best apple pie, chili, or chocolate cookies and hungry runners flock to Casey's to enjoy their efforts.

The members of the club have been powerful enablers of my running addiction. Once I started to spend a lot of time among runners, I started to accept things as normal behavior that used to seem unusual, things like getting up early to run 20 miles in a downpour.

When I'm away from home and my friends, whether I'm traveling for work or for vacation, running is a good way to get to know my destination. I can run by myself, or I can get out and meet other runners by entering a race or showing up for a run hosted by a local club or a running store. Runners are everywhere, so there's usually something going on.

Almost anywhere I go, I can find a local Hash House Harriers kennel to run with. Hashers call themselves a "drinking club with a running problem". There are thousands of local hashes all around the world. If I want to find the local hash, I can check the Internet for schedules or ask the drunkest person at any post-race party.

Some hashes focus more on running, others more on socializing and drinking. There are cities with multiple hash groups and runs almost every day of the week. Anyone with a thirst for beer and a taste for harmless juvenile behavior is welcome to drop by.

Local traditions vary, but hashes usually follow a similar

pattern. Each week, one or more "hares" plan a new trail and announce the location where trail begins to the rest of the pack. When it's time to run, everyone gathers at the start to socialize, and maybe down a beer or two. The hares leave to mark their trail, and after a little time passes, the rest of the group (the "hounds") head out to track the hares by following their trail marks. Usually, the trail is deviously marked in a way that forces the fast runners to slow down and puzzle out the true trail. That keeps the fast runners from getting too far ahead of the slower runners and walkers.

Each trail has one or more "beer checks", where the pack stops to rest, talk, and quench its thirst for beer. At the end of the trail, more beer is consumed, silly (often profane) songs are sung, and there's food (and more beer).

Going to a hash is a good way to find some fun and get some exercise too. Hash often enough and you may get your very own "hash name", usually something you wouldn't want to share in polite company. If you do go to a hash after reading this, when you're asked "Who made you come?" (you will be asked) be sure to say that "Boner in the Circle" sent you.

I started hashing on business trips, then spent a few years regularly attending my local hash in Boston. I've followed (or set) trails in some unusual places, wearing (or not wearing) unusual gear. I've run:

- On rocky trails well over a mile high in Colorado, where I was complimented as "a pretty good runner for someone from sea level"

- Through the desert outside Las Vegas

- On the same weekend as I ran the marathon in Boston and Burlington, without skipping the pub crawl

- Through a 100 foot drainage tunnel and across a sign maintenance catwalk over Interstate 5 in San Diego

- Naked, in the woods in VT and on a ship in Boston Harbor

- In a red dress, running with hundreds of other hashers through Washington and Boston

Wherever I went, I met fun people and found copious amounts of beer.

Sometimes, business travel leaves me in a place where the running isn't terribly pleasant. I'll be in a hotel surrounded by office parks and other hotels on a boring grid of wide streets filled with cars constantly streaming by at high speeds. The only place to run is on the hard concrete sidewalks, with nothing to look at other than the signs on the buildings as I pass by. Even so, there can be little touches to make the running something more than just keeping in shape. I might find a nice little restaurant tucked in among the offices that I might otherwise have missed, or a railroad right-of-way that has been converted to a multi-use trail. I fondly remember coming back from a run in the Virginia heat and being greeted by the Ritz Carlton doorman with a towel and an icy bottle of water.

Other times, I can find better places to run with a little effort. I used to travel to the Washington, DC area regularly for work. If I was there on Tuesday nights, I took the Metro into the city and ran with the Potomac Runners. Their group meets at a parking lot near the Capitol and heads out for a 6-8 mile run. The Washington Monument, Lincoln and Jefferson Memorials, Reflecting Pool, and other historic monuments provide unique scenery along the way. I needed that sometimes, to distract me from the swampy DC summertime weather.

Another business trip took me to San Diego, where it was consistently sunny (after the morning haze burnt off), dry, and between 65 and 70 degrees. I went there for a conference, and I extended my stay so I could run in the Rock and Roll

Marathon the following weekend.

When I checked the Web for interesting running groups and places, I found a trail running group that ran on Sunday mornings from the Movin' Shoes store in La Mesa. They met at 7AM, which wasn't too early for me, since I was still on Eastern Time.

The Sunday I ran with them, we went out to the Cuyamaca Rancho State Park. The park had recently reopened following some massive wildfires the year before. It was a good hour away from the city, but it was worth the trip.

San Diego is a port city, but as soon as you drive away from the ocean, you're climbing up into the mountains. By the time we got to the park, we were up around 4500 feet, well above the morning clouds that covered the city. It was a beautiful day for running, sunny and in the 60s.

This was the first time the group had been back to the park since it had reopened. There were four of us: me, the organizer from the store, and two regulars. We headed out on one of the main trails, where we met a couple of park rangers on horseback. They warned us to stay on the trail since the park was still recovering from the fires. We assured the rangers that there'd be no problem, but what we didn't know was that we were about to run out of the section of trail that had been restored after the fire.

We ran across a meadow, and then the trail began to get more "natural". Since there hadn't been much rain, in many places the underbrush hadn't grown back. This made hard to pick the approved trails from the surrounding dirt. Soon we were off trail, bushwhacking uphill while wading in a soft, deep mix of dirt and ash.

The runners who'd been there before were amazed at how things had changed. The fires had consumed most of the park, and blackened trees were everywhere. The underbrush that had grown back was well fertilized by the ash and much taller than usual. The wildflowers were sparse, but colorful and intriguingly different from what I was familiar with back east. Once we'd climbed for a while, we had magnificent views of the park and the Laguna Mountains, with colors and shapes nothing like what you see in New England.

We finally gave up on finding more trail and worked our way down to the road so we could get back to where we'd left the car. It ended up being about a 9 mile run, mostly at an 8-9 minute pace, with numerous pauses to figure out where we were and to stare at the scenery.

When we got back, we were all a dusty grey from the waist down from the ash. One of the guys told me to be sure to wash well when I got back. It turned out that we'd been running through another plant I wasn't familiar with: poison oak. I was warned not to scrub too hard, so I wouldn't rub the poison in, but I looked down and saw I had a number of bloody scratches from running through brush, so the poison oak was already in if it were ever going to get in. I ended up with a mild rash, but the trip was worth it.

Another time, Ruth and I went on a week's vacation to Bar Harbor on Maine's Mount Desert Island. We checked the Internet and found the Crow Athletics Running Club site. When I posted to their message board to ask about runs, they told me that some of the Crows were getting together in the town center on Friday the week we were there to run the start of the Special Olympics torch relay. I decided I'd meet up with them and run with the torch for a while.

When I got to the run, Crows Gary Allen and Peter Keeney were there. Gary is heavily involved in the local running scene. He's the director of the MDI Marathon, and he's the sort of person who runs 100+ mile weeks while living on an island that has only 3 ½-miles of paved road. Peter, another running fanatic, had run the entire 65-mile torch relay the previous year. Luckily for me, the Bar Harbor police chief and a few of his officers were also there to support Special Olympics. The run would be at a slow pace to accommodate the police, whose lives didn't necessarily allow them the time for a lot of training.

We ran from Bar Harbor, across Mount Desert Island, and off the island to Ellsworth. A support van with an enormous electric sign saying who we were followed us. The van carried food and drinks and was there for any runners who needed a rest. Gary, Peter, and I made things easier on the rest of the group by passing the torch between us while we ran and told running stories.

In Ellsworth, there was an exchange point with more food and drinks. The Bar Harbor police dropped out and other officers joined in as the relay headed on towards Augusta. The Crows and I kept going for a total of 30 miles. Then we let the relay go on without us while we called in for a ride back to Bar Harbor.

Florida is one of my least favorite places to run. It's hot, and in many areas all the available routes are straight, flat, and boring. Runners go out early in the morning or late at night to avoid the heat. A lot of them wear jackets to protect them from the "cold" temperatures in the mid-60s, something I always find amusing.

On one business trip to Florida, I entered a "Beat the Sheriff" 5K. The race started at dawn, so I had to get up early to get there in time. It was worth it, since I finished third in my age group. My prize was a bronze medal shaped like a sheriff's badge. At the airport baggage check on the way home, security pulled me aside and I had to open my bag and show them the medal. They were concerned that it might be a ninja throwing star or some other weapon. Good thing this was well before 9/11.

On another Florida trip, Ruth and I were visiting her mother at the same time they happened to be holding the 4th Annual Turtle Trot 5K. We signed up and were joined at the 7AM start by Ruth's brother Matt. The race is run on trails in Lover's Key State Park. The course was flat, except for a "38-foot mound" that the race organizers warned everyone about. Good thing they did, otherwise we wouldn't have noticed it (it's no Winter Hill). On the other hand, it was humid and well into the 80's, the no-seeum's were out in force, and I had taken most of the previous month off due to an injury, so we weren't expecting to take full advantage of the flat course.

The race was chip-timed, so the results were up quickly. Ruth finished in 26:55, 6th of 35 in her age group, and one place ahead of her brother. I ran 22:44, which put me third in my group, in line for a medal. I had my modest face all ready to go as we waited on the beach at the finish for the awards ceremony. Unfortunately, there were some late registrants who were hand-timed, and when they added in those results, I ended up 4th out of 20. No medal for me.

Winning a medal would have been nice, but I do what I do for all kinds of reasons, and not necessarily for reasons that matter to anyone else. I run for the comfort of cruising yet again through mile six of my familiar 12-mile loop, the wonder of running parallel with a deer on a path across a West Virginia field in the early spring or watching the fog roll in through the open bar door after a San Francisco hash, the excitement of standing knee-deep in a flash flood while holding onto the aluminum poles of the timing tent in a lightning storm or dodging snowplows on the run in a snowstorm, and even for the struggle of running a 10K in the heat of an Indiana summer. Whether I'm at home or on the road, the more I run, the more reasons to run I find.

Ray Charbonneau

My shoe rack

Chapter 3: Stuff - Shoes and Clothes

"I started running when I was 42 because I found footwear that I liked to run in. I always thought I hated running. Really, though, I just hate running shoes. I grew up mostly barefoot, and I just really hate shoes."
- Steve Kleindler

Runners don't need a lot of clothing. Competitors in the Olympic Games in ancient Greece ran barefoot and naked. That tradition continues to this day. Sometimes it's a planned event, like the assortment of "Bare Buns" and "Dare to go Bare" races, or sometimes it's spontaneous, like when the beer is flowing and a Hash House Harrier decides to take advantage of the freedom of running trail naked in the woods.

I usually wear a little more than that when I run. Actually, I'm a little obsessive about my gear. I'm going to run no matter what, but wearing the right gear when I run makes running a lot more fun.

At a minimum, I put on a pair of running shoes, shorts, and a T-shirt before I go out. I have additional clothes piled up in a closet for the times when the weather requires it. None of it is particularly stylish, and some of it has gotten sort of ragged, but we've gone through a lot together, and I'm too sentimental (and cheap) to toss things aside while they still have life in them.

It starts with the shoes. The right shoe is a very personal choice, and it's the most important choice a runner makes. There is an enormous array of shoes available, which makes it hard to find the best pair. A good shoe will make your running smoother, faster, and more injury free. But the wrong shoe is an expensive torture device.

I always take the time to turn my shoes over and shake any debris out of them before I put them on. Otherwise, I'm likely to end up with a blister caused by a small piece of gravel or a stick that got in my shoe on my previous run.

I tie my shoes snugly, but not too snugly. I used to wonder why the tops of my feet hurt after I had been running for a few miles. I added cushions, and that helped some, but finally I figured out that I was tying my shoes too tight. My feet swell after I've been running for a while, and if my laces are too constrictive, they cause pain. But if my shoes are too loose, my feet slide around inside them and I get blisters. It took me a long time, probably longer than it probably should, to get the laces right.

When I was in high school in Vermont, there were few choices. It was before hundreds of thousands of people started running marathons and before running shoes became popular for everyday wear. The shoes that were available were all very basic designs. I ran in Nikes, but back then, Nike shoes had none of the Air or other expensive gadgets that they sell today. The Cortez trainers that I bought were just about the only thing available in the local sporting goods store. Their soles were only slightly thicker than the lightly used Boston racing flats and Americas spikes that I raced in, which were handed down to me from teammates on the track team. Today, just the idea of running in something as stripped-down as the Bostons or a track spike makes my body cringe with potential pain.

When I returned to running in my early 30's, Nike Air was in the air. The first shoes I chose were a pair of Nike Air Pegasus, partly due to the ubiquitous Nike marketing juggernaut and partly because of the sentimental attachment to the brand that I had from high school. Unfortunately, before too long one of the air bladders developed a leak, so I decided to try another brand. By this time, the running shoe market had exploded in size, and picking a shoe was more difficult. Consumer Reports recommended the Saucony Jazz, and since I wasn't yet aware of how ridiculous it was to pick one "best" shoe for everyone, I tried a pair.

After I ran in the Jazz for a little while, I started showing some physical wear and tear. My issues started with plantar fasciitis pain in my heel, and moved on to illiotibial band problems in my right knee. I kept trying different shoes, looking for a solution. Some attempts worked better than others.

I figured that since I was getting more serious about running, I could justify trying the most expensive shoe. After all, the shoes that cost the most must be the best. So I moved back to Nike and up to their top-of-the-line model, the Nike Air Max. They had elaborate gas-filled bags in the midsole designed to provide durable cushioning and lots of it. In theory, since the shoes were extra durable, they'd last longer and I'd get my money's worth.

In order to get that extra cushioning, I had to accept the Nike fit, which was too tight around the forefoot. When I started to wear the shoes, I got blisters on almost every long run. I stubbornly tried different pairs of socks, various kinds of padding and bandages, and Vaseline and other lubricants. I spent a lot of money on those shoes – they had to work!

Finally, I gave up on the cool shoes and started wearing shoes that weren't as "technologically advanced", but were wide enough for my feet. Now I replace my shoes more often, but I get many fewer blisters.

I've run in shoes from New Balance, Adidas, Asics, Reebok, Newton, Merrill, and Salomon, in addition to other models from Saucony and Nike. I've tried on shoes from even more manufacturers. Essentially, I've paid for a number of expensive shoe buying lessons. At times, it seems like I've tried every gimmick available on the market in the hopes that I'd finally find the tweak that would solve all my problems. Most of the gimmicks fail.

Even now, after numerous false hopes, I'm still on the lookout for the perfect running shoe. Lately, I've run a lot in Mizuno Wave Riders, a neutral shoe that has decent cushioning and an upper that gives to make room for my wide feet. But I still try other models. I'm like an alcoholic who tells himself that the next drink will be the one that finally makes everything better. Unfortunately, there is no miracle shoe that will resolve all my aches and pains.

I haven't given up. If there is a perfect shoe out there for me, I won't find it unless I'm willing to try new things. I guess I'm an optimist after all. Or just gullible.

Lately, I've been trying shoes designed to help get me off my heels and land more on my forefoot with my center of gravity ahead of my landing point. In theory, if I do this right, it'll help reduce the frequency of my injuries. One shoe I'm trying has extra forefoot cushioning and very little heel cushioning. Another has hardly any cushioning at all. A rule of thumb estimates that an ounce of shoe makes a difference of about two seconds per mile to a racer. That adds up to almost a minute per ounce for a marathon. That's just the sort of advantage I'm looking for, one I can get without any need to train harder or longer. These shoes might be another waste of my time, effort, and money, but if so, it won't be the first time.

I try out a new shoe model for a while before using it in a race. Any problems with the shoe are magnified under the extreme stresses I subject it to when I'm racing.

Whenever I do find a good shoe, that's when the shoe company changes the design or discontinues the model altogether and forces me to start my search again. I'll always be looking for the right shoe for as long as I keep running.

I usually have at least three or four pairs of shoes going at any one time. I always have a couple of pairs of whatever my main running shoes are at the time so I can alternate between them when I run. My shoes last longer when I allow enough time to let them dry thoroughly and let the cushioning decompress between runs.

Some people recommend that you alternate slightly different models of shoes when you run, so you subject yourself to slightly different stresses each time you run. In theory, this reduces the risk of repetitive strain injuries. In practice, I have enough trouble finding even one shoe that I can run in comfortably, so once I find one that works, I stick with that model.

In addition to my main shoes, I keep at least one pair of trail running shoes around. These shoes have outsoles with a tread designed to provide more traction on slippery surfaces and a firmer midsole/outsole combination for more protection when I'm running on rocks and other rough surfaces.

I always have at least one additional pair of shoes. They're the shoes that seemed like a good idea when I tried them in the store, but turned out to be wrong for me once I took them out for a longer test run on the roads. A key to avoiding injuries is to identify those poor shoes as soon as possible and get rid of them. Unfortunately, I'm too cheap to throw a $90 pair of shoes away immediately. I'll keep them around for months, and give them multiple "last chances" before I finally give up on them.

Another key to avoiding injuries is to get rid of worn out shoes instead of trying to squeeze a few more miles out of them. I keep track of how far I've gone in each pair of shoes in my running log. Knowing how long it took to wear out earlier pairs of a shoe model helps me judge when it's time to replace my current pairs. Another rule of thumb is that a shoe is good for about 500 miles, but I usually find I'm better off if I get rid of them before then.

I use my running shoes for running and nothing else. My expensive shoes break down much faster if I wear them all day. I wear an old pair when I'm walking around. My shoes always have plenty of life left for walking after I'm done running in them.

I go through new running shoes a lot faster than I use the old ones up for walking, so I donate the extra pairs to charities. The mistakes that I can't run in are especially good candidates for donation, to ensure I get rid of them before I hurt myself trying too hard to get my money's worth out of them.

I wear whatever shoes I'm using year-round, no matter what the weather. Unfortunately, choosing the rest of my clothing isn't as simple. I need to pick the right clothing for each day's weather to maximize my running enjoyment.

One of the interesting things about running is how it changed my relationship with the weather. 75° (Fahrenheit) and sunny is not a beautiful day anymore. Instead, it's too hot for a good run. On the other hand, 48° and cloudy is not just a cold and dreary day, it's also a great day for a long run.

When I started running, it was springtime and I was only running a couple of miles, so I could get away with wearing cotton gym shorts and a t-shirt. Then winter came, and I started buying clothes specially designed to keep runners warm. Now I have closets full of the stuff. Whether it's 85° and sunny or -40° and windy, I can go out for a run.

The longer the run, the more important it is to choose the right clothes. Good running gear fits properly and is made so there are no seams, labels, or rough materials in a place where they will grind against my skin and make a rash or draw blood. If I plan ahead, I can use Vaseline or some other anti-chafing lubricant to guard against excessive friction. I can put band-aids on my chest to avoid the dreaded bloody nipples. But I'd rather get clothes that don't cause problems in the first place. It's no fun to get in a shower after a run and have the hot water hit a raw spot. It's even worse if the friction is bad enough that I notice it while I'm still out running.

Most of my running clothes are made from synthetic fibers with a weave that wicks sweat away from my body and helps the sweat evaporate faster. Synthetics dry faster when I'm done running, and smell better while hanging on my drying rack.

The right materials help keep me dry, but no matter what clothing manufacturers say, there's no such thing as a miracle fabric that is both wind-proof and breathable. Back when I started running, I lusted after one of those Gore-Tex suits that promised to keep me warm and dry in all kinds of weather. I found one on sale for half-price and bought it, but I was disappointed. It worked great to protect me from wind, but it was usually too warm to wear in rainy weather. I had a choice - go without the jacket and be wet from the rain or wear the jacket and be wet from sweat.

The Gore-Tex suit wasn't a complete waste of money. It wasn't warm enough by itself in colder weather, but for many years it served as my outer layer on cold, windy days. In retrospect, I should have known. How can any outfit keep wind from getting in, but still let water vapor out? Air molecules are much smaller than water molecules, and are much less likely to attach themselves to nearby surfaces. The best I can do is to try to manage the balance between wet/hot and dry/cold by choosing my clothing. When it's hot, I want to maximize air flow to increase evaporation, to keep myself cooler and dryer. As it gets colder, I need to reduce the air flow to stay warm, but I still need to carry as much water away from my skin as possible, and I need to let that water evaporate, or else my clothes will get soggy. But if I allow too much vapor to get out, that lets the cold air get back in.

My gear goes through a lot with me. I get emotionally attached, and I keep it longer than I should. I kept that Gore-tex jacket until all the waterproof coating had worn away and there were huge rents in the side where water bottle belts had worn through. I'd probably still have it if the pockets hadn't torn open. Another time, I accidently melted my first polypro hat in the dryer. I searched and searched until I could find an exact replacement, though there were lots of other hats readily available. I guess I wanted to make it up to that hat's family or something.

I live in New England, and I run when I travel, so I need many different outfits to deal with all the possible weather conditions. Luckily, once my friends and relatives figured out that running clothes were usually a good gift idea, my supply of gear built up quickly. And for some reason, I often find perfectly good winter hats while I'm out on a run, maybe because of the respect I paid my first hat when it died. A trip through the laundry and into the pile they go. I've also found a couple of pairs of expensive Oakley sunglasses. When I'm spending my own money, a $12 pair will do just fine, but free isn't bad either.

I've reached the point where I don't actually need new stuff that often, especially since the synthetic fabrics that running clothes are made of don't wear out as quickly as cotton. The few times I do buy something, it's usually online or discounted in a store or at a race. I have splurged and paid the full, somewhat exorbitant price for a jacket at my first Boston Marathon and a fleece shirt at my first Vermont 50, but I don't actually run in those. Their sentimental value as mementos of major events and the effort it took me to get there outweigh the cost and their usefulness as running gear.

As I gathered more stuff, it became important to have somewhere to keep everything so it didn't take over my living space. When I bought my first house in 1994, I found an old armoire in the basement that the previous owners had left behind. That armoire made an ideal running closet. I've used it for that ever since, taking it with me through a divorce and three moves.

I keep a drying rack and a shoe rack next to the armoire. That's enough storage space to keep the gear I'm currently using organized in one place in the house. The off-season clothing gets stored in the basement. Sometimes a pair of tights or a jacket will find its way into another part of the house for a while, but Ruth understands when that happens. Her gear doesn't always make it back where it belongs either.

I've got:

- Two visors, including a Newton Shoes freebee

- Two moisture-wicking baseball-style caps, one from the appropriately named HAT 50K trail race, and one from the Cool Running web site which was my first payment for writing about running. Ruth has claimed the Inov-8 Shoes hat I picked up at the Stone Cat ultramarathon, and the host of cloth caps don't count.

- Two "desert caps" with flaps that cover my ears and neck during long runs on hot, sunny days

- A pile of sweatbands I use on my wrists and head

- Two wicking stocking caps, one a little heavier than the other

- A couple of fleece stocking caps that I found while out running (I've never actually had to buy one)

- A fleece balaclava

- A neoprene face mask, which I only use in the most extreme cold

- A pair of lightweight wicking gloves

- A pair of fleece mittens

- Seven singlets, including three different styles of singlet for the Somerville Road Runners (my club), a Saucony singlet from my stint as a model for their Boston Marathon ad campaign in 2005, and an Asics singlet that was the first running gift I ever got

- Two wicking sleeveless shirts, including one from GAC, the club that I ran with in some trail ultras

- Two wicking short-sleeve shirts (plus too many cotton t-shirts to count. I give a trash bag full away every year)

- Four (more or less) wicking lightweight long-sleeve shirts

- Two wicking medium-weight turtleneck shirts

- Three heavier-weight wicking mock turtleneck shirts with fingerless gloves built into the end of the sleeves

- A fleece vest

- A couple of fleece long-sleeve shirts

- A heavyweight fleece hoodie

- A nylon vest

- A water-resistant nylon jacket

- Another nylon jacket that's bigger, so it fits over multiple layers of clothes on cold days

- A windproof fleece jacket

- Six (more or less) pairs of shorts

- Three spandex tights, including one in SRR colors
- Two fleece tights
- One pair of nylon pants
- One pair of waterproof pants
- A pile of jocks
- A pile of synthetic running socks

Did I say I had enough clothes? Maybe I understated things a little.

I don't insist on fresh clean clothes on every run, except for socks and jocks. I don't always smell great, but I don't have to do laundry every other day either. When I do get around to the laundry, I never use fabric softener or dryer sheets. The chemicals stay in running gear and clog the weave, reducing their ability to wick sweat away. I'm too lazy to separate the running clothes so I can use fabric softener with my regular clothes, so we just live with the static cling. Unfortunately, synthetic running clothes are especially static-y after going through the dryer.

When I first started running in the winter, I wore too much. I bundled up enough so that that I was fairly comfortable when I stepped out the door. But when I warmed up after I started running, I'd get too hot. I'd start unzipping and taking things off to cool down. But by then I was already sweaty, so when I let the cold air in, I'd be cold and damp instead of hot, and I'd get even more uncomfortable.

Over time, I learned that I could get by with less clothing. I'm still adjusting my choices. Every year I wear a little less when I go out for a run in the cold. I suffer a little more at the start, but that just encourages me to get going and generate some heat. Still, if I have any doubt about how to dress, I always err on the side of "too warm". I can unzip or take layers off once I'm out, but I can't add anything if I'm too cold. And when it's <u>really</u> cold, my only concern is making sure I dress warm enough.

Socks and jocks are simplest to pick. I can wear the same ones in all types of weather.

I always run in socks made of synthetics, never in cotton or wool. They're medium-thickness, with a bit of extra material at the ball and heel where there's the most stress. Thicker socks don't provide any real additional cushioning, and my feet always generate enough heat to stay warm no matter how cold it gets. Some people prefer to run in thin socks or no socks at all, but I get more blisters that way. I've tried fancy double-layer socks, but they bunch up and cause more blisters than they prevent.

I always wear a jock strap. Even more than the rest of my running gear, my jock needs to be made with smooth materials and seams so it doesn't chafe, especially around the pouch. Regular jocks for football or baseball won't work. I had a favorite brand, but they went out of business and I had to search the Internet for a replacement. I found a number of web sites with a wide array of jocks, briefs, and thongs for athletic use. After perusing these sites for a while, I couldn't help but notice that there was another use for these that I was oblivious to. Besides keeping men comfortable during exercise, jocks are also good for "lifting and holding you forward when you go out for a night on the town." I only wear mine while I'm running. In the unlikely event that it happens to attract anyone, they'll have to catch me.

About half of all runners couldn't care less about jocks. They have a different concern, one that I'm unqualified to write about. My friend Sarah Fisher, a women's running coach and an experienced runner herself, had this to say about sports bras:

"When I became a runner, I discovered the sports bra and its many ways of humbling a woman. A sports bra is every woman's most important and valuable piece of athletic equipment, a necessity regardless of her size and shape.

"Bouncing boobs are both uncomfortable and attract WAY too much attention. The compression bras that are really tough to get into – and out of – do the best job. How did I finally find the right sports bra? By asking other women and trying on numerous styles until I found one that did the job. A few contortions removing a sweaty sports bra pale in significance if the blasted thing does its job. Now I can run with minimal bounce, while attracting minimal amounts of hooting and finger pointing, and without feeling like my breasts will rip right off my chest."

The rest of my outfit depends on the weather. When it's warm out, 60 degrees or over, I wear as little as possible. I'm a guy, so there's no illogical cultural bias that forces me to wear a shirt on a hot day. Even so, I usually wear one, mostly to keep my water belt from grinding against my skin, but a shirt also lets me go into stores, bars, or restaurants when I need to find a bathroom.

My tops are made of special materials that "wick away" my sweat and help keep me cooler. The advertising claims might be true this time, for all I know. I suppose a good singlet might make me a tiny bit cooler than bare skin. The weave in the singlet presents more surface area to the air than smooth skin does, and that could increase the rate of evaporation and do a better job of keeping me cool. Still, whatever wicking that occurs can't matter all that much. I sweat enough that after a short time, anything thin enough to be comfortable is completely soaked through.

I try to avoid running when it's really hot, 80° or more with a strong sun, by running early in the day or late at night. But sometimes that's not possible. Some races are held during the day in mid-summer. If it's a long race, like the SRR 24 Hour Around the Lake Relay, I actually wear more. I cover my top half with a light-weight, light colored (preferably white) long-sleeve shirt and one of my desert caps with the neck and ear flaps. The white clothes reflect some of the sunlight and keep me cooler, the same way a Bedouin's robes keep him comfortable in the desert.

When it's hot, I avoid cotton or any other materials that absorb water. Cotton is soft and comfy when it's dry, but when it gets soaked with sweat it gets wet and heavy and it chafes. If the temperature gets below 60°, that's cool enough so I can get away with wearing cotton t-shirts on shorter runs. Sometimes I'll wear a t-shirt if I like the message printed on it, or because it reminds me about a favorite race or a PR effort, but usually I wear t-shirts just so I can conserve laundry by wearing yesterday's shirt on today's run before I put it in the wash.

When the temperature drops to around 50°, I start worrying about being too cold. A long-sleeve shirt is usually warm enough. Sometimes I'll layer a short-sleeve shirt over that. Cotton shirts work surprisingly well for this second layer. The first layer carries my sweat away, and the cotton layer soaks it up. The sweaty cotton actually helps block any wind. As long as I keep running so my body heat keeps the inside shirt warm I stay comfortable.

The colder it gets, the more important it is to choose the right outfit. I have three different types of long-sleeve shirts that I'll use for a base layer. As the temperature gets lower, my long sleeve shirt gets thicker. When it drops into the 40s, I start using the mid-weight shirt. Into the 30s, and I add my nylon wind-proof vest as an outer layer and start wearing a lightweight hat and gloves.

Around 30°, I start using my "windproof" fleece jacket for my outer layer. Windproof fleece has a tighter weave so it blocks more air, though not as much air as a nylon shell. Regular fleece lets too much air through to use as an outer layer. By itself, the windproof fleece is still not warm enough if there's a strong wind, but in most weather it creates a good compromise between wet and cold.

The trick is to have a thick enough layer of wicking clothing so there's room for a temperature gradient between me and the outside world. I want sweat to pass through to the outside where it can evaporate, so I'm not weighed down by soggy clothes. But I want to trap enough heat so my body can keep the inner layer of sweaty clothes warm. I know I'm wearing too much when it's below 40° if I can stand outside comfortably for more than a minute or two when I'm not running.

I have a thin uninsulated windproof shell for times when it's windy enough to be a problem. I can use that thin outer layer more often than an insulated shell. If I need more warmth, I can always add another layer of fleece underneath the shell.

It usually gets warmer during a three-hour morning run, so the clothes that were right at the start are too much by the end. During any run, the sun comes and goes, hiding behind trees, buildings, or clouds. Winds rise and fall and swirl from all directions. The effective temperature can change 10-30 degrees or more in the course of a run. It takes judicious use of zippers to stay comfortable.

My legs generate a lot of heat when I'm running, so dressing my lower half is less complicated. I wear shorts until it gets down around 40°. When it gets colder, I replace the shorts with spandex tights. Some people find that spandex reveals things they'd rather not reveal. Tights add warmth without too much bulk, and that's more important to me than what I look like. I add shorts over my tights, but only when it's cold enough that I need to keep important things frostbite-free.

When it gets even colder, the layers get thicker. I live near Boston now, and the ocean keeps it from getting really cold most of the time. I grew up in Vermont, where it gets bitterly cold on a regular basis. The coldest weather I've gone running in was in Vermont when it was 20 below with a wind chill of -40. I was fully decked out, wearing:

- A Neoprene facemask
- A fleece balaclava over that
- A fleece hat over that
- A thick fleece long sleeve shirt
- A fleece vest over that
- Polartec's thickest fleece hooded sweatshirt over that, with the hood over all the other headgear
- A jockstrap
- Spandex tights over that
- Fleece pants over that
- Spandex gloves
- Thick fleece mittens over those
- And a windproof nylon jacket and pants over everything

I wore my normal socks and running shoes. My feet never get cold while I'm running.

I could barely move with all this stuff on, and the ice that formed on the inside of the neoprene mask from the moisture in my breath got pretty nasty, but I was warm enough to get my run in.

In a cold weather race, I wear a little less than usual since I'll be running hard the whole time. That makes it very important to time my pre-race warmup correctly so I don't spend much time standing around sweaty and cold before the race starts.

Most of the time, rain is nothing to worry about. I'm going to be wet with sweat, so rain is just more water. The only change I make when it's raining is to wear a visor to keep the rain out of my eyes. My body heat keeps me warm enough as long as it's above 50°. When it starts to get colder, I'll wear a little more than usual to ensure I stay warm. A water-resistant layer won't really keep me dry if there's more than a sprinkle of rain, but it'll be wind-resistant enough to trap body heat if I'm standing around in the cold while I'm wet for some reason. Anything that's really waterproof is too uncomfortable to run in.

My least favorite running weather is when the temperature is in the upper 30s and it's raining. It comes as a relief when it gets a little colder and the rain turns to snow.

Some runners strap cleats on their shoes when they're running in snow or ice, but I don't bother. The cleats are uncomfortable to wear on hard surfaces and don't help my traction that much. I just run more carefully when it's slippery.

My clothes are a random mix of styles and colors. Choosing my clothes based on appearance always seemed pretty silly to me. Why should I care if I'm color-coordinated when my hair is pasted to my head with sweat, crusty dried salt is all over my face, and I smell like a gym locker? I worry about having bright clothes with reflective patches that are easy for drivers to see, not whether I'm running in gear with matching colors and labels from the right brands. Clothes are for protection and comfort. And I always get my money's worth out of my clothes. If I were concerned with appearances, I'd have to replace my clothes before they wore out, rather than wearing them until the rags fall off my body during a run.

The only clothing item I bought for appearances sake is my running club singlet. When I'm going to a race, I wear my club singlet even if I have to wear it over thick layers of winter clothes.

I do have one rule regarding style. Whatever I do, I do not wear the commemorative shirt from a race in the race! That would mark me as a new runner, and is just not cool. If you aren't going to wear a club shirt or technical running shirt of some kind, shirts from other races are OK. Any of these are better than the shirt from the race you're running:

- A shirt from a previous edition of that day's race, the older the better

- A quirky shirt from a race that's obscure because of its size or location

- A shirt from a well-known far-away race

- A shirt from a race where you set a PR (personal record)

- A shirt from a well-known race

- A shirt from an alternative kind of event (trail races, triathalons, etc.)

Any of these shirts provide entertainment for other runners and give you something to talk about. I wear my club singlet during the race, but I'll break out one of these after the race, when I change to dry clothes. The shirt from the race I'm in stays packed away, unless it's the only dry shirt I have. Of course, there are other kinds of shirts that aren't from races, but I have so many free race shirts that they've driven most of the other shirts out of my closet.

I go through all this because the right clothing helps make running fun, even in bitter cold. In 2007, my high school friend Mark was training for his first marathon. He was running Vermont City in the spring, so he needed to train through the winter. Ruth and I were visiting in Vermont a little before Christmas, so we all planned to go out for a 15-mile run one Saturday morning. It was -2° when we met near the airport in Berlin to go out to run. It wasn't windy, so we put on our thick layers of polypro and fleece, and skipped the wind layer.

It was a beautiful day with a bright sun. Soon after we started running, we were warm enough to be comfortable. Two colors dominated – the blue of the cold, clear sky and the white of the unbroken expanses of snow that covered the fields. The grey stubble of leafless maple trees on the mountains and the drab rundown rural houses added a dour touch, but there were other splashes of color – Ruth's bright orange hat, the Christmas decorations on the houses, and the dogs frisking in the snow, hoping to play as we ran by.

We powered along, chatting or listening to the crunch of the light layer of snow beneath our feet. The only visible clouds were frozen vapor from our breathing. Our clothing kept us comfortable most of the time. The only chill came when we passed through the shade cast by thickets of trees.

By the time we were finished, we each had an extra layer of icy fleece woven from the crystals of sweat that had wicked to the surface. Ruth had lacy tendrils of ice coating the curls of hair peeking out from under her hat to accent her outfit.

A week later, Ruth and I were in Florida visiting her mother at Christmas time. It was 85° and sunny. That wasn't bad either.

On the trails in West Virginia

Chapter 4: Stuff – Gadgets and Gear

"I discovered that running with an iPod for entertainment turned an attitude of, "oh no, I've gotta go out and run," into, "hey, running further gives me more time to catch up with favorite podcasts"."
                    -Tim Cooke (McCavity)

The right equipment adds to an addict's enjoyment as he satiates his craving. A drunk prefers a particular style glass for his scotch on the rocks. Pot-smokers have elaborate bongs to cool their smoke. In the 80's, cocaine users wore their little spoons on a chain around their necks.

Running addicts are the same way. To feed my running habit, I've accumulated all sorts of gadgets intended to help me run better, keep closer track of how much I'm running, and magically cure what ails me. I'd like to think that every item I picked was sensible and a good value, but sometimes a gizmo ends up staring down at me from a shelf, a baleful warning against wishful thinking.

I'm not saying running gear always has to be practical. If it's a cool toy that's fun to play with, I'm happy. Running is supposed to be fun.

Sunglasses mix the cool and the practical. A good pair of sunglasses is important for comfort and protection on sunny days, and stylin' in the right pair makes me look and feel fast, or at least makes it a little more convincing when I tell myself how fast I am. I usually buy cheap sunglasses. They work just as well as the fancy ones and they don't make me cry when I lose a pair. I did pay a lot for one pair of sunglasses. They're the ones with the prescription I need to read course maps and fill out race applications now that I'm getting older.

I do a lot of running on city streets where there's a lot of traffic. For safety's sake, it's important to be visible to others at all times, especially in the winter when ice and snow block the sidewalks and narrow the roads. My running clothes and shoes have reflective patches on them, but that's not enough. When it's a gloomy, cloudy day, I wear a bright orange reflective vest. At night, I add clip-on lightweight flashing lights. I may not look stylish, with orange mesh layered over my mismatched running clothes, accented with portable disco lights, but I will get the attention of any drivers as they pass by me. Even so, it seems like no matter what I wear, drivers still seek me out. Maybe I've crossed a line to where I'm so annoyingly bright that my gear turns drivers into motorized moths mindlessly chasing my blazing image.

On most runs, I need something to drink. I might go 3 or 4 miles without a drink in the summer, and maybe stretch that out as far as 6 miles in cooler weather. But for anything longer, I'm going to want some fluids to keep myself hydrated. I've tried fancy drinks laced with special electrolyte mixes and protein, but at the core, I'm lazy so I usually stick to something that I can get anywhere easily and doesn't need mixing before I can use it. Water is good enough on shorter runs. I use Gatorade on longer runs where the additional carbohydrates and electrolytes are useful.

I have a belt that I use on short runs that holds a basic 20 ounce plastic bottle. For longer runs, I have some backpack-style Camelbaks, rated to hold 50, 70, and 100 ounces. None of them actually hold quite as much fluid as they say they do. And I can never use all of the capacity they do have. When I try to squeeze those last few ounces in, they come right back out as soon as I try to screw the cap onto the bladder.

Even my largest Camelbak doesn't hold enough to last me through an entire long run in the middle of the summer. If I run out of fluids on a run, I can refill with tap water from a bathroom sink a water fountain, or, if I'm desperate, someone's outdoor hose faucet. Tap water doesn't taste great, and sometimes it gives me an upset stomach. I try to refill while I still have a little Gatorade left, to help hide the taste of the tap water.

I prefer to stop at a store and buy a sports drink if I can. My stomach is happier, and I also get the benefit of a short rest while I shop. In the places I run most often, there's always a store within a mile or so when I need one.

On a hot day, I put in some ice before I go out to keep my fluids cold as long as possible. A cool drink is more refreshing when I'm on a run, and cool fluids are absorbed into my system quicker to help me stay hydrated. Ice cubes are better than nothing, but I found a special tray that makes long, thick tubes of ice. Those ice tubes fit easily through the mouths of my containers, and they last a lot longer than small ice cubes.

In the winter, the problem is keeping my sports drink from freezing. I'll use Gatorade more often because the minerals in it helps keep ice from forming. When it's really cold, I wear my Camelbak under my outer shell, so my body heat keeps the fluid a little warmer. Everything tastes a little like body, but it's enough to keep ice from forming in the bladder or clogging the drinking tube.

Camelbaks are a pain to keep clean, but if I don't wash them regularly, mildew grows in the nooks and crannies. I keep my Camelbaks in the refrigerator between runs to slow down the growth of the gunk, but eventually they need a thorough cleaning. My pile of gear includes custom brushes for cleaning the bladders and the drinking tube, bleach pills to kill the mildew, and a rack that fits inside the bladders and hold them open so they can dry.

I usually carry other miscellaneous items on a run in

addition to my sports drink. I always (unless I forget) have a key to get back in the house. I usually have a pocket to stash the key in, but if I don't, I tie it on my shoelace. On a longer run, I might need to find storage space for:

- Some cash, for fluids or post-run snacking

- Painkillers. I used to take ibuprofen regularly, before and during runs, but now I try to stick to Tylenol to save my stomach

- Anti-histamines or an EpiPen. I'm allergic to insect stings, and I'd rather not die on a run.

- Energy gels, and a sandwich bag to keep the empty packets from getting everything sticky

- My public transit pass, in case a long run goes bad (haven't used it for that yet!)

- Band-aids, for blisters

- Butt wipes, in case the need arises and there's no toilet paper

I carry a selection of this stuff in my jacket pockets or in a small zippered belt pouch.

Sometimes I need even more stuff than usual, or I'm running to work and I want to carry items that are too big to fit in a pouch or pocket. That's when I use the 100-ounce Camelbak. I usually don't need that much to drink, but the bag is a backpack that's large enough to carry a change of clothes and any other items that I'll need, like my wallet and my eyeglasses.

I have a waist belt I use for long trail runs that fits somewhere in between my usual water belt and my large Camelbak. It holds two 20-ounce water bottles and has a pouch that's bigger without being too big, enough for a few additional things I might need for trail running, like a flashlight and batteries, extra blister protection, or snacks.

Every runner has a sports watch. Every year, at least until I break down and start running in my prescription glasses, the size and readability of the display on my watch becomes more important. I can still read the display on mine without my glasses, but I can't read the labels on the buttons, so I only use a few functions while I'm running. My watch has a stopwatch I use during races, and a repeating countdown timer I use to time my stretching routine and to time intervals when I'm training. I can set my watch to repeat intervals that are all the same length, or to repeat sets of unequal intervals when I want to do 5 minutes of running followed by 1 minute of walking. The watch also has a second time zone and an alarm clock that I use once in a while when I'm traveling.

My watch is also the display for a heart rate monitor (HRM), which provides an objective measure of my level of effort when I'm training. A chest strap transmits a signal to my watch, which displays my current heart rate. I can set my watch to beep when my heart rate gets out of the optimal target zone for the type of training I'm doing. There are a number of different methods for estimating those target zones, which implies that using a HRM for training may not be quite as scientific as it seems. Still, a HRM helps keep my effort consistent, especially on hot days when it takes more effort to run at a particular pace than it does on a cooler day.

I used to use a HRM more often, mostly to ensure that I ran my easy runs at an easy level of effort. Once my runs got long enough, it became almost impossible to keep my heart rate below the desired level without walking, especially when I was going uphill. I didn't have the patience for that, so I put the HRM aside.

Sometimes I wear a GPS watch to measure my runs. I'm

on my third different model of GPS. My first one had a cumbersome separate receiver pod that transmitted data to a watch, but now the entire GPS system is housed in the watch. It's a little clunky on my wrist, but I've got my eye on the next generation, which has shrunk to the size of some regular sports watches.

Before I had a GPS, if I wanted to know how far I was running, I had to measure it on a map or drive the route to measure it with the odometer. I usually ran the same routes, adding together shorter loops to make a long run. The GPS gives me the freedom to go out for a ten or twenty mile run without having to plan the route in advance. I can head off in any direction and run wherever I want and still get an accurate measurement of the distance to put in my log. Sometimes I use that freedom to sneak in a few extra miles, and that makes me feel virtuous.

My GPS watch doesn't do everything I need my watch to do, so sometimes I end up with the regular watch on one wrist and the GPS watch on the other.

My most important piece of running equipment, other than my shoes, is my portable music player. Music is an energizer, a soundtrack for a heroic effort, or an end in itself. I like listening to good music almost as much as I like running. If I combine the two, I get a lot more time to listen to music than I would have otherwise.

When I have the opportunity, I enjoy running and talking with other people. When I'm racing, that takes all my attention. The rest of the time, I run with music.

Music distracts me when I'm tired or bored or in pain. That's good, as long as I don't get so anesthetized that I let my form get sloppy or ignore a pain long enough to let it become an injury.

A radio won't skip while I'm running and I don't have to

load it with what I want to hear. But I'm picky. I can't tolerate a lot of popular music, and inane commercials, DJs, or talk show hosts drive me crazy. I always bring along something that lets me play my own music.

The first player I ran with was an original Sony Walkman cassette player (remember cassettes?). Cassettes were cheap and easy to use, they didn't skip, and I could create my own tapes from my collection of vinyl albums. However, the songs on a cassette always played in the same order, cassette tapes regularly got sucked into the works of the player and mangled, and carrying multiple tapes and spare batteries on long runs was inconvenient.

Portable CD players sounded better than cassettes, but they skipped at the tiniest jostle, and this was back when it was inconvenient to burn my own mixes onto CDs. Instead, I replaced my cassette player with a MiniDisc player (remember those?). MiniDiscs were smaller than cassettes and CDs, the player ran longer on one set of batteries, and the discs sounded better than cassettes. I could play the songs on a disc in a random order. The player did skip from time to time, and dealing with multiple disks was still annoying.

Then I got my first MP3 player. It was a 128MB Rio 800. It was small, and I bought the optional snap-on 128MB "backpack" to double the storage so I could load it with 3 or 4 hours worth of music, enough for all but my longest runs. I loved my Rio, but it had problems. Music files loaded slowly through its USB 1.0 interface, and the Rio froze up when it tried to play certain songs. To reset it, I had to unsnap the backpack to disconnect the battery, and that was hard to do even when my hands weren't sweaty or covered with gloves.

I wanted more storage so I wouldn't have to reload after every run so I could play different songs. I tried an Archos Jukebox with a 20GB hard drive, but it was big and ugly, and it jammed the first time I took it on a run. I exchanged it for a boxy little RCA player with a matchbook-sized 1.5GB hard disk. The RCA carried plenty of music and loaded faster via USB2, but the music management software for my computer and the controls on the player were cumbersome.

The cool people were buying iPods. Initially, I resisted getting one. For a time, iPods were a Mac-only product, and I was a Windows guy. Then Windows connection kits appeared, but iPods were big and expensive, and I didn't trust the hard disk to stand up to the pounding it would take when I went running with it.

I got tired of trying to manage my MP3s with Real Jukebox, Musicmatch, and the other applications that worked with my RCA player (and don't get me started on Windows Media Player). I found a plug-in for iTunes that let it work with the RCA, so I loaded iTunes, took a look, and liked what I saw.

Then I went into a store and picked up a second generation iPod nano and fell in love. It felt just right in my hand – next to Ruth, the nano might be the sexiest thing I've ever run with. It was easy to use and iTunes made it easy to load with whatever I wanted to hear. Once I replaced the 50-cent earbuds that came with it with decent headphones, it sounded great. The nano became my constant companion on the road.

Soon after I bought the nano, Apple announced the 2nd generation of their entry-level Shuffle player. When I saw it, I immediately lusted after one. It was tiny, cheap enough, and came with an integrated clip that removed the need to put it in an annoying case before I could run with it. The Shuffle was supposed to be ready in October 2006 but it didn't show up in Apple stores until November, so the staff in the local Apple store had to get used to me calling to ask whether it had arrived yet. When the Shuffle was finally available, I went to the store to check it out and it was just as cute as I thought it would be. But since I didn't *really* need it, I held off on pulling the trigger. Then Apple came out with colored cases early the following year and my resistance crumbled.

The Shuffle can go anywhere. I can stick it in a pocket or I can clip it to my collar, the shoulder strap of my Camelbak, my hat, or my sweatband. Then I'll tuck the headphone wires out of the way and head out for my run, unencumbered by straps, cases, or bulky players.

Those iPods met my needs. They didn't hold all my music, but they were easy to reload, and I still didn't trust the hard drives in the high-capacity iPods to hold up to accidents or the pounding of running.

There was one thing that was a problem. Sometimes I run intervals to work on my speed or to stretch out my long runs by switching between running and walking. My watch signals the end of an interval by beeping. The problem was that I couldn't hear the beeps over my music.

I tried removing the watchband from an old watch and wearing the watch near my ear, tucked under my hat or my sweatband. I could hear the beep over my music that way, but it was uncomfortable, the watch often fell out, and I couldn't see the watch when I wanted to glance at the time.

Ideally, I wanted my iPod to time the intervals and play a signal through the headphones when one ended. The nano (and the other iPods, except for the Shuffle) already had a stopwatch. But it was a crappy stopwatch that only had simple start, stop, and split timing functions. For some reason I had to pause the timer before I could stop it. And the stopwatch wouldn't let me recall my splits when I'd finished running.

Then Apple came out with the iPod Touch, a version that was their popular iPhone without the phone. The Touch is programmable, so it runs all sorts of applications in addition to playing music. When I looked in Apple's App Store, I found someone had written an interval timer that could play its beeps over my music. The timer app was only 99 cents. Unfortunately, the Touch was quite a bit more. But now I have a third iPod.

Runners think nothing of planning out a day-by-day training program geared towards a race a year away or tracking exactly how many miles they've run in a pair of shoes. I'm equally obsessed with choosing the right music to bring on my runs. I've ripped my favorites from my collection of about 2,000 albums to MP3, and I regularly download new songs from the Internet to add to my virtual pile of bits.

Some people string together playlists to act as the soundtrack to their own personal "Chariots of Fire". I tend to pick a group of songs and let them play in a random order. The surprise helps keep things fresh.

Everybody likes to run to up-tempo, anthemic songs that inspire you to pick up your feet, and the pace. I also like slower, steady songs that lend endurance by getting into a groove that just keeps rolling along, like "The Rail Song" by Adrian Belew or "Marquee Moon" by Television.

There are songs about subjects that remind me of running, like "Running up that Hill" by Kate Bush, "Everybody Hurts" by REM, "Feel the Pain" by Dinosaur Jr., and "Born to Run" by Bruce Springsteen. A few songs are actually about runners. There's "The Stars of Track and Field" by Belle and Sebastian, "Like a Rock" by Bob Seger, and, um....

None of the songs I just listed were made after 1998. I'm getting old.

When I'm fully loaded up for a run, with drink carriers, iPods, sunglasses, multiple watches, lights, and everything else, I sometimes look as ridiculous as the White Knight from "Alice in Wonderland". But when I run without all that junk in a race, I feel like I can fly. Sometimes I'll sign up for a race just to enjoy having someone else there to serve me a drink every mile.

I've got an entirely separate pile of running gear that never leaves the house. It's the stuff I use to prepare for runs, recover from runs, or keep track of what I've been doing.

I keep my running log in an Excel spreadsheet on my computer, replacing the paper notebooks and journals I used to use. I note the distance for every run in my log, but only to the nearest mile. I also enter the basic type of run, whether it's easy, normal, or hard, and I note which shoes I was wearing, so I can tell when they're due for replacement.

Compared to many runners, I don't actually track that many things. I skip many common items, like route, weather, time of day, how I felt, and so on, but I'm obsessive about what I do track. Excel adds up the weekly, monthly, yearly, and lifetime totals for me and creates graphs, so I have plenty of ways to look at my progress (or lack thereof).

I only log the time for a run if it's a race. Otherwise, I'll always be competing, trying to run faster every time. That's impossible, and I don't need any extra ways to lose, or to injure myself.

In 2002, I logged all the money I found while I was running. I always stop to pick up loose change, unless I'm in the middle of a race. When anybody asks, I tell them if I'm in too much of a hurry to stop and pick up money, I'm going too fast. Most of the money is in pennies, but every once in a while I'll find some silver. The total for the year I kept track worked out to be exactly $4.

Google and the Internet have replaced magazines as the source of answers for any question I might have about running. Notice my use of the plural. For almost any question, I can find multiple, often contradictory answers somewhere on the

Internet. That's part of the fun.

I can search for races and plan running routes wherever I happen to be, shop for gear, and look up information. I also use the computer to keep in touch with my running friends via email, mailing lists, Facebook, and blogs.

Reading is probably my favorite way to entertain myself when I'm not running, so I've collected a number of books on running. Some are informative. For example, I found the first "Galloway's Book on Running" to be useful when I was starting out. Tim Noakes' "Lore of Running" has almost too much information, perfect for an obsessive runner like me. I have other books that are intended to be entertaining or inspirational, like "The Runner's Literary Companion" and "Running Through the Wall". Since you're reading this, you probably have your own collection.

I do some basic strengthening so my body holds up better for running (or biking, kayaking, or skiing). I mostly do situps and other things that don't require equipment, but I have some weights, an exercise ball, a rubber mat, and a few other odds and ends. I used to have a treadmill, but I never learned to like running without going anywhere, so it ended up as an expensive clothes-drying rack.

Sadly, too often my preparation fails me or I overdo it, and I end up with an injury. When I can't run, I get a little desperate, so I've bought a variety of tools that were supposed to help me keep on the roads or heal quicker so I can get back out:

- Foot orthotics, to help optimize my alignment

- Massage tools, like The Stick (a flexible rolling pin), a few spiny massage balls, a foam roller, and a Thera-cane,

- A balance disk, sort of a flat exercise ball, for low-back exercises

- Night splints, to keep my foot flexed at night to help with plantar fasciitis

- Ice packs

- Neoprene knee braces

- Compeed blister protection pads, that I ordered from England once they stopped selling them in the US

I'm very susceptible to snake oil cures, so I also have a collection of less useful items in the bottom of my closet. These things may or may not work, but at least they keep me busy when I can't run.

My final essential piece of equipment is a belt. Not a belt for carrying water on a run, but a regular belt, the kind you use to hold your pants up. I use the belt to monitor my weight. If I have to let the belt out a notch, it's time to start running more or eating less. Most people use a scale to monitor their weight, but I don't think there's a need to watch my weight that closely. I already have plenty of things to obsess about.

Not all races are on the roads

Chapter 5: Injuries – When Denial Fails

"Something that I learned by sitting on barstools is that if the stool is narrow enough you can straddle the stool and while drinking your favorite brew you can massage out those tight adductor muscles. If you drink enough while straddling the stool, when the adductors let go you'll see, rather feel, how those muscles deter you from sitting or standing up to your full height. It may take a few bars and a few brews to find the right barstool. It is well worth the effort."
-Ozzie Gontang

Running is good for me. Running helps me manage my weight and my blood pressure, builds my strength and endurance, and works to prevent cancer, osteoporosis, and other diseases. My dad had his first heart attack when he was about my age, but my running should help fend off heart problems. A good run relieves stress and can help manage depression. Humans evolved to be good long-distance runners because ancient man hunted for food by chasing animals until they dropped from exhaustion.

Running is bad for me. Studies show that in any one year, 60-80% of all runners have to take time off because of an injury. Running damages my joints and strains and tears my muscles. Running is stressful. The running writer Jim Fixx is just the most famous person to die of a heart attack while running. Running generates free radicals, which have been linked to cancer. Another famous running writer, George Sheehan, died of cancer. Ancient hunter-gather humans lived short lives compared to today's humans.

I really don't care. For me, the enjoyment I get from running outweighs any possible negative impact on my health.

Running is an addiction, but it's usually a benign one. Maybe I'm just an endorphin junkie, but I always feel good after a run.

When my running is going well, I train harder and race more and enjoy every minute of it. Unfortunately, I inevitably push too hard, overdo it, and end up injured. When I can't run, I don't get my endorphin fix. The fact that I can't run because of an injury shatters the illusion that I have control over my running. I'm told that I get cranky and irritable when I'm hurt. I don't notice it myself. I'm too busy wondering when I'll run again.

I try to avoid pain and injury as much as I can so I can feed my addiction. That means taking care of myself before, during, and after each run.

Good health for runners starts with the sorts of things that everyone should be doing, whether or not they're a runner. That means eating right, drinking plenty of water, and getting plenty of sleep.

I try to eat right, to consume more whole foods and fewer sugary, salty, or fatty processed items. Unfortunately, no one has made a vegetable that tastes as good as bacon or ice cream. Part of the reason to run is so I can eat what I want and not get fat. And I want cookies!

Beer and coffee have water in them, right? I don't drink anymore, but I haven't noticed my running getting better because I quit drinking. I was known to have a beer or two in the middle of a run and three of four afterwards. The Tarahumara Indians of northern Mexico are supposedly the best distance runners in the world, and much of their culture revolves around massive consumption of corn beer.

My morning coffee is one of the highlights of my day. The active ingredient in coffee, caffeine, is addictive, so that first cup is just quenching my withdrawal cravings. Still, some studies indicate that coffee actually improves performance. A cup before I run can help me use fat for fuel, release calcium stored in my muscles to help me run farther or faster, and give me the energy to get going and keep me alert and focused while I'm running.

Of course, nothing is perfect. Coffee can act as a diuretic, though the effect is minimal for regular coffee users. The acids in coffee help cause acid indigestion and force my body to use extra minerals to keep my system in balance. Coffee can also leave me jittery and interfere with my sleep, especially if I have any late in the day. And if I miss my daily dose, I get cranky, tired, and headachy.

When I'm not drinking coffee, I usually drink water. I have a soda (never diet!) once in a while, but soda is one place where I have successfully cut down on my sugar intake.

I try to balance healthy eating and comfort foods. It's more important for me to enjoy life than it is to maximize my potential as a runner. No diet is going to make me an Olympic-class athlete or even a regular winner at local races. Most of the time, the food I eat supports my running. When it doesn't, I eat the lobster with butter and fried onion rings guilt-free, and I just go for another run to make up for it.

Sleep is different. I'd love to sleep more, but it's not really something I can make myself do. I get up at more or less the same time most mornings, I try to avoid napping during the day, and I let the rest take care of itself. Quitting drinking has helped here. I'm much more likely to make it home at a reasonable time so I can get up and run the next day.

Most runners do more than just eat and sleep properly to help support their running habit. It's easily possible to spend more time preparing to run and recovering from running than you actually spend running.

Everyone – runners, doctors, therapists, little old men smoking at the lottery counter – says you need to stretch in order to run well and stay injury-free. But no one agrees on the best way to stretch. Do I spend 10 seconds, one minute, 15 minutes at a time on each muscle? Stretch before or after running? Hold a stretch, or repeatedly swing to the limit of my range of motion? Stretch sore and injured muscles, or leave them alone? Everyone has a different opinion.

I think stretching for runners may be a plot created by people who are flexible enough to actually enjoy stretching. I'm not. I do some stretching anyhow, partly because it does seem to help me retain the little flexibility that remains in my legs, but mostly so when my doctor or therapist asks me if I stretch, I'm not lying when I say yes.

I've tried yoga classes, and I've enjoyed them up to a point. Since I lack flexibility, I get quite a workout as I struggle to get into my best approximation of the correct pose. An hour of yoga, with all the meditation and controlled breathing, is relaxing in spite of the strain. But it comes down to a choice between spending my time on running or yoga, and running always wins.

Massage is another form of therapy that many people use. Unlike stretching, getting a massage feels good, and I definitely feel better after I've received a massage. My legs might be a little sore right after a deep-tissue massage, but after a day or two they usually feel fresher and ready for more hard training. The main difficulty with massage is the expense. A good hour-long massage costs as much as a decent pair of running shoes. It's worth it, but the price does add up.

I have a foam roller, a "Stick," and some other self-massage tools, but they never seem to work as well. Partly, I expect, because I don't spend as much time with them. Fifteen minutes with the foam roller is tedious. An hour with a good massage therapist is heaven.

I suppose stretching and massage do some good, because

so many people do them. However, when scientists study the effects of stretching or massage, they never find conclusive evidence to show that they actually do anything to help people run better or prevent injury. I love seeing those studies – they help justify my lackluster approach.

Many runners work to develop strength with exercises and weightlifting. Stronger muscles are supposed to help runners maintain good running posture longer and be more resistant to injuries.

I have about 20-30 minutes of exercises I do a couple times a week, mostly sit-ups and other exercises designed to maintain strength in my core muscles. A strong core helps me protect my back and keep good form while I'm running.

I've tried some weightlifting, particularly when I was doing a lot of trail running. The main effect was that I gained weight. It was muscle, but the muscle didn't seem to help much with running and it certainly didn't protect me from injuries, so it was just more weight to carry around. On the other hand, eccentric weightlifting -- extending muscles under load rather than contracting them -- has seemed to help me recover from nagging injuries.

I do other sports for fun that happen to be good cross-training for running. Biking and cross-country skiing help build strength and endurance while giving me a break from the pounding I get when I'm running. Kayaking is great for developing my core muscles, though my tight runner's hamstrings sometimes make it difficult to sit in the boat for long periods.

Some people go so far as to compete in these other events, or mix them together in multi-sport "athalons" of one form or another. They're forced to spend time cross-training, when they could be running, if they want to be competitive in multi-sport events, and that's not for me. Also, it's hard enough to train and use whatever natural physical ability I have when I'm competing with others. If I need to buy better gear to help me to improve in a sport, staying competive on that level can get expensive. So I'll stick to buying running shoes instead. Anyhow, I prefer running. Biking for transportation and swimming to cool off are enough for me, thank you.

I do some things before I go for a run to help avoid discomfort while I'm out, especially when I'm going on a longer run.

I use a stick lubricant on sensitive areas, like my inner thighs, to reduce chafing. People used to use Vaseline. Races would often have someone at aid stations holding a sheet of cardboard coated with Vaseline so runners could scoop some off on the way by and use it to coat any sort spots. Today, there are products available that do the same thing, but last longer and are not as messy.

I might stick a band-aid or an anti-blister pad on spots that tend to get blisters. My feet have gotten tougher, and blisters are less of a problem than they used to be, but when I'm going on a long trail run, I still need something to protect my feet.

A long time ago, the goodie bag for a race I was in came with a sample of a product called "Compeed" that was great for preventing blisters or protecting blisters while they healed. A Compeed pad stuck to my foot through the stresses of running better than anything else, especially if I helped it with a little tincture of benzoin. Then the brand was bought by Johnson & Johnson. They relabeled the product with the Band-Aid label, and then watered them down over time until they adhered no better than anything else. When my little stock of real Compeed was running out, I turned to the Internet in desperation. I found that they still sold the original version in England so I ordered a quantity of the good stuff by mail. I still have some left more than six years later because I hoard them, using them only in marathons and other long races.

In the summer, the heat and the sun add to my problems. I put a little round band-aid on each nipple to keep them from chafing against the lightweight mesh shirts I wear when it's hot. I have some electrolyte capsules I bring with me on long runs on sweaty days when a sports drink isn't enough to keep me from cramping. Sometimes I even remember to put on sunscreen.

Some of the things I use to prevent pains before a run, like stretching and massage, also help me to recover from any discomfort that persists after a run. If I apply ice to sore muscles, that brings down the swelling and dampens the pain, and I hardly ever get frostbitten skin. Soaking in a cold tub right after a long run is a good way to reduce inflammation and speed my recovery. I only do that in the summer. I'm not going to hop in a cold tub after spending a couple hours outside on a New England winter day, no matter how much it might help in the long run.

Running helps runners retain our youthful appearance, but in another way, it makes us more like old people. Just like the elderly, when runners get together, a main topic of conversation is our health and our aches and pains. There's always plenty to talk about.

No matter how much I prepare, running still hurts. The hurt that comes from extending my limits and pushing through simple tiredness to go faster or farther is a good hurt. Unfortunately, there are always other pains unless it's a very short run. A toe joint complains, my lower back protests, a hamstring rebels – every body part has chimed in at one time or another.

Running through those pains has taught me to pay no attention to little things. Many non-running injuries can be ignored. I know runners who have run after shoulder surgery

Ray Charbonneau

with their arm still in a sling and runners who've run with their broken arm in a cast. After I had my own shoulder surgery, my doctor said I could do whatever I wanted as long as I could tolerate the pain. That was good enough for me. I took off the sling and went for a run. He had no idea how much pain I'll put up with in order to run, but I wasn't going to straighten him out.

Another time, I signed up for a 5K while I was on a business trip. The night before the race, I had a muscle spasm in my neck. I couldn't straighten my head, and the pain kept me from sleeping. The next morning, I ran in the race anyhow, though I couldn't move my head and it was locked at an angle that made it hard for me to run smoothly or see around some of the turns. My only regret was that someone I couldn't see passed me at end and beat me out for 2nd place in our age group.

I try to ignore illnesses too. I might cut back some when I'm sick, but I usually keep running, unless I have a fever. Sometimes running seems to help me burn out the germs and get better faster. But that's balanced by the times I get worse after running, and I have to dial it back further or even stop for a while. I may feel bad about taking the time off, but the forced extra rest sometimes ends up helping me out. In 2004, I was in bed sick for two days just before I ran the Green Mountain Marathon. That turned out be enough tapering off to help me finish in 3:26 despite little training and a sore hip.

The pains that develop while I'm running can usually be managed. A new pain means it's time to check my running form. I'll usually find I've let something slip, and when I correct whatever it is I'm doing wrong, the pain goes away, or at least becomes tolerable.

Sometimes nothing I do makes a pain go away. It keeps nagging at me as the miles pass. But if I keep going, sometimes a new pain arrives. The new ache sometimes almost serves as a welcome relief, by distracting me from the old one.

For a long time, I regularly took ibuprofen to help get me through my long runs. My hips and back often start to stiffen up and hurt somewhere around 10 miles into a run. That makes it hard to keep going even when I'm not tired. Vitamin I helped keep the pain and inflammation away. If I was going to run much more than 10 miles, I took ibuprofen before I started to delay the onset of the pain. If I was running far enough, I'd often end up taking some more during the run.

Too much ibuprofen can be dangerous. It's implicated in a long list of potential problems, including stomach ulcers, kidney problems, and hypertension. Tylenol is safer, but it doesn't have the same beneficial effect, presumably because it doesn't have the same anti-inflammatory qualities. I was willing to ignore the risks of too much ibuprofen, but after a while my stomach started to get upset from the pills. I mentioned that to my doctor, and he gave me a prescription for Celebrex. Celebrex didn't have the same effect on my stomach, so I began to take that before a run, though Celebrex was supposed to increase my chance of having a heart attack or stroke. Again, I chose to ignore that risk so I could run with less pain.

I finally worked my way up to a case of acid reflux disease. The painkillers probably contributed to that problem, so these days I'm trying to stay away from the pills as much as I can.

Another reason to back off on the painkillers is that they can make it harder to tell the difference between pain and injury. The trick is to decide whether a new pain is just another ache and I can safely run through it, or it's a serious injury that needs treatment or, even worse, rest. That can be a very hard choice to make, especially mid-run, when I'm used to pushing through pain to get to the finish. If the pain is muted by ibuprofen, it's harder to make the correct decision.

From time to time, someone trips over a rock and breaks a leg, or tears an Achilles while sprinting, and no matter how tough they are they have to stop and get the problem taken care of. But most running injuries are not caused by a traumatic event. They're due to wearing down from repeated stress, not a single blow.

I usually find out I have an injury when the pain doesn't go away after a run is over. If a pain is still there when it's time for the next run, the prudent choice is to postpone the run until the pain goes away. It's that simple for a lot of people - if something hurts, don't run. Of course, I never do *that*. The problem is, if I don't run when something hurts, I'll never run, and that's not acceptable.

Sometimes ignoring the pain works, sort of. The pain persists for days, weeks, months, or in some cases years, but it never gets so bad that I can't run. The balance between the physical discomfort from the pain versus the mental discomfort of taking time off to heal never tilts far enough in the direction of rest to get me to stop running.

My right Achilles is a typical example. For years, it's been creaky, especially in the morning. The tendon catches against the sheath when I get out of bed and walk. The problem fades away when I'm not running much, but it always comes back when I build up the miles again. It loosens up when I move around, and it usually doesn't bother me much when I run, but it's something that I worry about. Not enough to do anything about it, but...

Sometimes ignoring problems is stupid. I have hemorrhoids, which bleed a little from time to time. I was taking a medication whose side effects caused the bleeding to increase in frequency and amount, but I ignored the problem and kept running. Running got harder, and I almost quit before I went for tests and found that I had lost enough blood to become anemic.

When denial doesn't work, sometimes rest helps. That's how a runner defines a serious injury – it's a problem that keeps him (or her) from running.

When I do have to stop running, the tricky part is making sure I rest long enough. For example, I had an illiotibial band problem with my knee that kept me from running. I'd rest for a couple of days and it would feel fine. Then, when I tried to run, the pain came back after a mile or so, and I'd be forced to walk home. I finally had to take a couple of weeks off to let it heal for good, but I spent a couple months messing around before I could make myself leave it alone for that long.

It's hard to stop eating like a distance runner when I'm forced to take time off. It still takes the same size portions to satisfy me, even though I don't need as much fuel. Weight starts piling on when I'm not burning 3,000 to 5,000 calories a week by running. Non-runners start telling me how healthy I look, because I've lost my usual gaunt, desiccated appearance. I don't gain extra weight quickly, but it's still a problem. Luckily, the stress and anxiety of worrying about gaining weight helps me burn some of those extra calories.

Taking time off because of an injury does make me realize just how much time goes into running. All of a sudden there are extra hours in the day that I need to fill with some kind of activity. Normally I'm not much of a TV watcher, but during one month-long stretch of downtime while recovering from a nagging hamstring injury, I discovered Turner Classic Movies. I watched a lot of old movies that I had never made time for before, like "Casablanca," "Roman Holiday," and "The Philadelphia Story". Audrey Hepburn and Cary Grant helped fill the days, but once I could run again, the TV went back off. Even Audrey can't compete with running.

The extra time I have when I'm not running does give me more time for cross-training while I recover, if the injury permits it. When the weather's cooperating, I've got time for more spur-of-the-moment skiing or kayaking. Yoga classes also help pass the time, as long as the injury doesn't keep me from struggling into the poses.

I try to use cross-training to keep my fitness up for when I return to running, but it's just not the same. Without a lobotomy, I can only do 10-15 minutes on an elliptical trainer or a stair-stepper. When I was training for my first marathon, I tried running in a pool to keep my weight off an injured leg, using a flotation belt to hold me upright. It was funny-looking to watch. All you could see was my head poking up from the water as I slowly traveled back and forth. Pool running was better than nothing and I did stay cool and comfortable in the pool while I was working out, but when I've had other injuries, without the desperate need to make it to my first marathon driving me, I've never gone back.

I usually bike just for transportation, but when I'm injured, I will do more biking just for the exercise. Biking is probably the best alternative form of training, but spending a lot of time on my bike mostly reinforces my preference for running.

My body usually heals with time and a little self-therapy. But if rest and treatment don't work, or when it's a traumatic injury and there's no other option, then it's time for me to visit the doctor.

Doctors are people too, with all that means. They can be just as kind, mean, diligent, lazy, happy, sad, smart, hungry, tired, or distracted as anyone else. Sometimes they're right and sometimes (hopefully not often) they're wrong.

I work with my doctor, but I keep my mind working too.

He (or she) is the medical expert, but I'm the expert on how I feel and how I'm reacting to treatment. That's important too. I also have more time than my doctor, an Internet connection, and more reason to search for information specific to runners.

The first time I had plantar fasciitis, I found information on the use of night splints to keep my foot stretched and help relieve the pain. I took the information to my doctor. Today, you can order a night splint ready-made, but at the time, they weren't very common. My doctor hadn't worked with a night-splint before, but he thought it sounded like a good idea. He put a cast on my leg with my foot flexed, carefully cut it off, and fashioned a custom-fitted night splint that I wore in bed to help me recover.

I'm not always an easy patient. When I go to the doctor, I want the doctor to fix what's wrong, right now. I've already tried resting, stretching, anti-inflammatories, and everything else available to me. I want him to Do Something to get me back on the road right away, if not sooner. That's almost never possible.

Sometimes the cure for a problem is actually pretty simple. I've had a couple cases of persistent jock itch that I couldn't treat with over-the-counter medications. My doctor prescribed a simple cream that soothed the rash away within days. Another, more serious incident occurred when wasps stung me a couple times while I was running trail with the hash, and I collapsed from anaphylactic shock. Luckily, my friends were able to flag down someone with a phone and call an ambulance, and the EMTs and the emergency room staff were able to get me back on my feet in time to make it to the on-in party after the hash.

Other times, professional treatment helps, but it still takes time to get better. I've been dealing with a case "runners butt" for most of the last year. I first noticed a problem when I

Ray Charbonneau

didn't recover well after a 20-mile race, though in retrospect, the problems I had during the race were probably a sign of the injury. I kept running anyhow, limping slowly along for short distances, until I reached the point where I couldn't lift my left leg or sit for long without pain.

A couple of months of rest did not help, so I went to my primary care physician, who referred me to a series of other doctors. None of them were able to help, and nothing showed up in any of the various tests and scans I went through, though we did eliminate bursitis, arthritis, osteoporosis, and a host of other possibilities. For the most part they suggested treatments I'd already tried, like rest, ice, and anti-inflammatories like ibuprofen, and none of them worked.

When I was leaving one doctor's office after he failed to help and had given up, he told me that I should be grateful that "it wasn't a serious injury". He was allowed to live, but it was a close thing.

We finally settled on a diagnosis of hamstring tendinosis, which happens when tendons are damaged repeatedly and not allowed to heal properly. The tendon develops snarls and chokes itself rather than working the way it should.

I went to a pain management clinic. My therapist there used deep tissue massage and ultrasound to break up the crud and allow healing. I also visited a doctor for a few sessions of trigger point injections. The doctor felt along my hamstring for knots left behind by previous injuries. When he found one, he stuck it with a needle, wiggling the needle and injecting a saline solution to try to get the knots to release. The treatments helped restore flexibility to my hamstring. I could stretch farther and with more comfort after each session. I also added eccentric hamstring extensions based on research I found on the Internet. I'd lift the weight with both legs so I wouldn't strain the sore leg, and then I'd let the weight down with just the injured leg.

All this finally helped enough so I could get back on the roads. My therapist also introduced me to some exercises inspired by the Feldenkrais Method, a system designed to help people move more efficiently to reduce pain or limitations in movement and promote general well-being. I've incorporated some things I've learned into my running form, and I'm hoping that'll help reduce my chance of injury in the future.

There's still some pain, almost a year after the problem began, but I've been able to slowly build up my mileage.

One nice thing about running while recovering from injuries is that if I'm supposed to limit myself to 3 or 4 miles of easy running, I get the virtuous post-run "I did what I was supposed to do today" feeling without having to run far or fast enough to be tired. That's sort of like appreciating unemployment because I get to run whenever I want, but it's still true.

I'm trying to put more effort into managing my aches and pains and reducing the frequency of my injuries. The work I've done to build stronger muscles and improve my running form has helped some, though there are times when I get discouraged and think that I may finally have reached the time where I just can't run as far any more. If I run less and rest more often, maybe fewer of my aches and pains will turn into chronic problems. I'm not sure if that's a sign of wisdom on my part, or whether I'm just wearing down after years of struggling with injuries.

Maybe I'm learning from all this. Whatever. As long as I can keep running....

SRR medal winners at the 2004 Irish-American 5K

Chapter 6: Racing is a Rush

"My basic theory of running is, simply, this: The faster you run, the sooner you get to stop."
- Sarah Fisher

If running is my addiction, racing is when I mainline the strong stuff. There's nothing quite like the rush of pinning on a number and seeing how hard I can push myself to reach the finish line.

When I began running regularly in May of 1992, it was mostly so I could eat what I wanted and still keep my weight down. Within a month, after I knew I could get through a few miles without stopping, I was ready for more. Jogging in circles for fitness wasn't enough. I wanted to see how fast I could run.

I found a four-mile race in a running magazine that started in nearby Somerville at a bar called Khoury's. I ran the 4 hilly miles in 30:48, finishing 35th out of 85 runners. My lasting memories from the race were sucking in clouds of hot automobile exhaust from idling cars as I ran by, with their indignant drivers glaring from the front seat, and an annoying competitor who kept sprinting by me, stopping to walk and rest, and then dashing by again. Even so, while sipping my free post-race beer, I knew I wanted to race again, and do better when I did. I was hooked.

I ran another race in July. I bought my first running book, "Galloway's Book on Running", in August. I entered my first half-marathon in October and I finished in 1:48:19. Recently, I finished my 178th race, the 2010 Newburyport Spring Fever 5K.

For a well-adjusted person, a race is a way to get together with their running friends, experience the thrill of competing, and measure their progress as they strive to reach their potential. Only the gifted few are actually competing to win.

I may never be that well-adjusted. Just about the first thing I learned when I started racing was that I was never going to win the big race. I'm faster than the average person, but the people who win races aren't average.

I may not like that, but I've had to get used to it. I've lost hundreds of races. Literally. I haven't been the first one across the line since high school. And that was in the slow heat of the quarter-mile (it was a long time ago, before U.S. track went metric) in a dual meet in small-town Vermont.

It is true what they say – everybody who climbs off the couch and gets out running is a winner. In some sense. But another equally true cliché is that second place is just the first loser.

Racing is rewarding in itself. Otherwise, given my level of success, I would have quit long ago. A garden variety mid-pack runner like me has to find satisfaction in the act of competing, whether or not I win, in order to keep going. If I run well, don't get hurt, and give everything I've got to reach the finish as fast as I can on that day, that accomplishment is enough to make it a good day.

Even on a bad day, when I'm just chugging along to get to the free beer at the end, I'll find that my competitive urges kick in, and I'll break into a sprint to beat that fat guy or pass the nice looking girl I've been following the whole race. Sometimes, finishing 102nd instead of 103rd can be a great victory.

But I have had enough success to know that all else being equal, winning is a lot more fun than losing. So like all the other runners who chose the wrong parents or have jobs, families, or injuries that keep them from being that one guy (or gal) on top of the heap, I'm always looking for ways I can experience the joy and satisfaction of coming out on top.

One way I challenge myself is to race myself. Everyone can train harder, put in more miles, eat better, and strive to beat last year's time in the local 5K. This gets tougher as I get older, but I still think I have room for improvement. Even if I never beat my 5K personal best from 1992 (the one that was probably on a short course), I can still try to run better than I did in my last race.

That's OK, but.... I admit it. I want to beat people. Other people. I want to be the one who congratulates the lesser runners for putting forth a good effort. I want to modestly tell others that it was just a good day, and that some other time, I'm sure they'll come out on top. All the while, inside I'm dancing and shouting "In your face, slugs!" That doesn't make me a *bad* person -- as long as I keep it inside.

The key to achieving the victories we all crave is to find an environment that's conducive to your success. Look for races that play to your strengths and minimize your weaknesses. Maybe you're strong on hills or especially sure-footed on rough trails. Maybe you run best first-thing in the morning, or in the heat of summer. Maybe you're better off if you avoid races with free beer. Figure out what works best for you, search out the race that fits, and sign up!

Unfortunately, even in the perfect race for me, after a great season of training and a good night's sleep someone faster always shows up. I have to face it, that's usually going to be the case. Then I have to create the environment that allows me to succeed. Narrow things down, twist the rules if necessary (not too far!), get choosy enough, and I *can* be a winner!

When I joined the Somerville Road Runners running club and started running our free weekly fun run/race, I began to recognize other regulars who always finished at about the same time I did. I got to know them. I drank beer with them. I learned their kids' names. And I worked to beat them, as they worked to beat me. Some of them knew we were racing, others never knew that I was stalking them every Thursday night. Friendly races within the larger race can be a lot of fun.

If you try and try, and just can't beat your friends, sign up for a relay race with them and let the faster runners carry you to victory. Relay races are a nice break from the solitary routine of running. You get the pleasure of cheering a friend to success, and their success benefits you. If you choose your friends carefully, you'll be sharing the glory in no time. In 1993, I was the slowest person on the second-place Men's Masters team at a 65-mile relay race around Lake Winnepesaukee in New Hampshire. That's still one of the high points of my racing career.

The most common way runners increase their chance of success is by growing old. Age group awards were created just for this purpose. I might not be able to run with the young studs, but I can compete with other old farts like me. My goal is to keep running long enough to get to where I'm heading to the awards stand regularly. "Long enough" may mean into my seventies or later, but no one needs to know that there were only two other people in my age group, and one of them was using a walker.

Another way is to look for races with multiple events. Maybe a 10K with a 5K or a marathon with a 10K. The faster runners always go for the marquee event, leaving the other race open for me to sneak in and win. The last two awards I won at a race were both age group prizes in secondary races. Note: Don't go so far as to enter a race for kids – that would be tacky.

There are other categories to aim towards. Handicapped people tend to frown on people who walk up to register for the wheelchair division. But anyone can be fat. Heavier people can win races with Clydesdale and Filly divisions without having to beat the scrawny types who train on air and vegetables. You can clean up at both the awards ceremony and the post-race spread. Unfortunately, a lot of the Clydesdale prizes end up being won by tall, fit guys rather than short, fat guys.

There are plenty of other choices. Races have divisions for runners in red dresses, runners pushing beds, and even naked runners. Some people address the problem by creating their own division. At the 2006 Boston Marathon, two men juggled while they ran the course, competing for the title of "World's Fastest Joggler". They didn't have to race the other 20,000 entrants for that title. I imagine that they would have had to struggle to find a third competitor.

If all else fails, I go small. Any of the ideas I've discussed are more likely to earn me a coveted win if I apply them in a race where only 30 people sign up. When I'm on vacation in a rural area, I look for a race in a nearby small town. I try to find races that run on weekday mornings. I'll register to run early on New Year's Day. With the Internet, there's no excuse for missing out on those hidden gems. First place is first place – the trophy doesn't say how many people you beat. The best I've done is a fourth place finish (second in my age group) out of 32 runners at the Echo Lake 10-Mile Road Race in Charleston, VT. I haven't yet found a race small enough for me to win outright, but I'll keep trying.

If I can manage to combine a small race with bad weather, I've hit the jackpot. On a cold, rainy day, runners will stay home in droves. Sadly, I can never count on the weather to help me out. Even a New England February has some nice, warm, sunny days.

I've used many of these techniques, all that I can, and I

have accumulated a pile (albeit small) of hardware to show that they work. All it takes is a reasonable amount of training and an eye for an opportunity, and I end up with something to show for a race besides a t-shirt and sore feet. I can be a winner too!

Even when I don't bring home a prize, I usually leave a race with a concrete memento or two in addition to the more ethereal memories that I've created.

Almost every time I enter a race, I get a shirt. T-shirts promote the race, give sponsors, supporters, and charities widespread exposure, and they're fairly cheap to make. I haven't had to buy a t-shirt for years. I get enough of them from races to have some to wear, a few to keep for sentimental reasons, and plenty left over to donate to homeless shelters and clothing drives. Any experienced racer has a trash bag or two full of old race t-shirts. Some people have their favorite shirts made into quilts or get them framed. Most runners have a never-ending supply of cleaning rags too.

Lesser races provide "one-size-fits-all" shirts, and that one size is frequently the wrong size for the majority of runners. Better races put their logo on a moisture-wicking shirt or on one with long sleeves, or maybe even provide a hat or some other item of clothing instead.

Races often give runners a goodie bag, but they're usually filled with ads and other junk. There might be an energy gel or some useful snack food, and some of the big races have guides for runners that make nice keepsakes, but I usually end up tossing most of the contents by the time I get home.

I like to have pictures from races as souvenirs, especially pictures of me. Many races have official photographers, who take pictures of as many people as possible at multiple points in the race, then make the photos available for sale afterwards. I've ordered a few of these after memorable races, but they're too expensive to buy regularly. In New England, we're lucky to have Jim Rhoades and Ted Tyler, who take pictures at an enormous number of races and post them online.

For every race I run, I print one or two pictures of me from their site or the ones taken by my friends, and I save them in a race book, along with my race numbers and a note with my time. Every once in a while I like to flip through the book and look back. It's been gratifying to watch the book grow.

I have a collection of finisher's medals, mostly from marathons, that I hang on a tie rack. They make a satisfying jingle when I run my hand along them, though I have to be careful to keep from shattering the ceramic medal I got from the Derry 16-miler one year.

Then there's the finisher's award from the Nipmuck Trail Marathon. They painted a chunk of tree branch with a trail blaze mark and glued a label on it. It sits on a shelf, a miniature leaning tower of running.

There are other things that I've collected over time. These include SRR cowbells, a "No Parking - Marathon in Progress" sign from Boston, space blankets from various marathons, and a 3'x2' headshot of myself with my head uplifted in a "Soviet Hero" pose from the "Saucony 26" marketing campaign for Boston in 2005. I've also saved a SpongeBob SquarePants doll, badges, and a drinking game spinner from various hashes.

I even have a few prizes from placing in races. They don't take up a lot of space.

All these trinkets need a home. Lots of runners have a "me space" where they display their running booty. In our house, we combine the me space with the gear closet and the drying rack in a small room in the 2nd floor hallway. To keep us humble, we keep the cats' litter box there too.

One award is stored separately, in the kitchen. It's a glass cutting board decorated with a picture from a 50K trail race in West Virginia. That one was hard to get safely home on the plane.

Ruth is starting to accumulate her own collection of running mementos. She used to run in high school and college, and she got back into it after we met. Something about never being able to see me otherwise.

I suspect that for the most part, my fastest races are behind me. However, I've enjoyed watching Ruth as she goes through the initial stages of becoming a runner. She is just starting to find out what she can do. She keeps running farther and getting faster, and it reminds me of how good I used to feel when I was just starting out and reaching new levels of achievement with every attempt. I'm both happy and a little jealous that Ruth still has years of improvement ahead of her.

Ruth ran her first half-marathon at the inaugural Half at the Hamptons in 2008. It was an eventful race. For better or worse, she got to see the full range of what can befall runners when they put their training on the line and sign up for a road race.

The race featured a flat, fast course. The roads were mostly clear of snow. There was a wet snow squall that lasted about 20 minutes, but other than that it was a good day, if you keep in mind that it was February on the New Hampshire seacoast.

Ruth had a range of goals for her first half-marathon, starting with simply finishing the race. She was also targeting a 10-minute-per-mile pace, and looking to remain injury-free. Ruth succeeded in reaching all those goals and more. She ran a 2:06:33, which was a 9:40 pace. She ran hard, but felt she had something left in the tank at the end.

The overall winner was Daniel Princic of Woburn, MA, who finished in a time of 1 hour, 14 minutes, 57 seconds. Ruth was also a winner. Out of all the women in her age group, she was the fastest first-time half-marathoner. Her prize for that was a beer glass.

Most of the other runners had their goals, did the work to prepare, and when the race was over they ended up with a shirt, a finisher's medal, and the satisfaction that comes when your hard work pays off.

Some people didn't do as well. Maybe they didn't do enough work to support their goals, or maybe they misjudged their pace, started out too fast, and ran out of gas as the miles passed. Maybe they just had bad luck.

I was in that group. Somewhere after mile 10, my left calf began to hurt. I kept going, but it rapidly got worse. By the time I reached the 11-mile marker I had to choose between hopping on one leg for the last two miles, walking to the finish, or dropping out. There are races where I've walked longer distances to finish, but I like to think I'm getting better at taking the long view. In this case, it was cold and wet and I wanted to get to the finish to get some pictures of Ruth, so I caught a ride from a passing car and massaged my calf in relative comfort while I rode to the finish.

There were people who had much worse luck. One woman, Lynn Bova, had a very bad day through no fault of her own. I was standing about 10 yards past the finish, waiting for Ruth to arrive. During a lull in the stream of finishers, I noticed the scaffolding that was holding up the finish banner wobble slightly. I didn't see anyone leaning against it – maybe a gust of wind caught the banner, though for the most part, the high winds that were forecast did not show up.

When I looked back down at the course, Bova was approaching the chip sensor mats. From there, events proceeded too rapidly for anyone to do anything to prevent them. Just as Bova crossed the line, the top half of the scaffolding separated from the base and toppled sideways, carrying the whole structure over. People watching yelled for

Bova to look out, but she was concentrating on finishing her race. All she had time to do was look up before a crossbar hit her on the head and the falling steel knocked her down. Spectators pulled the scaffolding off her and took out cell phones to call in emergency medical support.

In the meantime, the race continued. Bova had to stay there, lying on the mat, while runners went by, because moving her might cause additional injury. I helped direct runners around where she lay, pointing them to the third of the chip mat that was still free.

Things settled down, and I moved back to where I could get Ruth's picture when she finished. Ruth was so focused on finishing that she barely noticed the group huddled on the mat as she went by.

I caught up with Ruth as she walked down the chute, basking in her personal victory. I helped remove her chip, and then we exchanged it for a finisher's medal and headed off to the car to get dry clothes. As we walked down the street, the rescue personnel arrived on fire trucks, sirens blaring. They took Bova off to the hospital. Later, race officials reported that she had needed surgery on her ankle, but that doctors expected a full recovery.

Another runner had the worst day possible. Fifty-five-year-old Bill Paradis collapsed about halfway through the race. Ruth ran by as people were performing CPR on Paradis by the side of the course while waiting for an ambulance to arrive. That's never a good sign, so she feared the worst. The next day, I read that Paradis was running with a friend when he complained that he couldn't catch his breath. Not long afterwards Paradis went down with an apparent heart attack. The paramedics were unable to revive him and he died. Paradis had run multiple marathons and was an avid cyclist. He knew what he had to do to be prepared for the half-marathon, but that doesn't always matter.

After the race, Ruth was caught up in the euphoria of her success. We went out for lobster, and the day was topped off when we were given number 1 for the number they would call when our dinners were ready. The next day, she wasn't excessively stiff or sore, and she was ready for an easy run on Tuesday.

I was happy for her, and her reaction helped me remember how rewarding it was to discover that you were capable of physical feats you thought were reserved for "real athletes". But I couldn't forget those who had found that tragedy can strike at any time, even at a moment of triumph, or in the midst of a pleasant diversion from your daily cares. The 2008 Half at the Hamptons was a clear reminder to live each day to the fullest while you can.

Running in a race is the purest form of competition. It's just me against the field, with a minimum of rules and equipment getting in the way. Other sports require teammates, expensive specialized equipment, or defined playing fields. The only other sport I can think of where the competition is as clear and straightforward as a footrace is boxing, but I prefer that all my physical pain be self-inflicted, so I'll stick to running.

A hard race is one of the few times when I am truly living in the moment. I'm totally absorbed in what I'm doing, not worrying about work or money or relationships. I might be suffering, and while I don't exactly welcome the pain, I'm not looking to be distracted from it either. I'm watching that pain closely to ensure I'm absorbing as much as I can, without redlining before I reach the finish. For as long as the race lasts, the only thing that matters is running as fast as I can, and trying to beat other people who are running as fast as *they* can.

There is a wide array of races, and each type has its own

feel. I like the relaxed and intimate atmosphere of a small-town race. The race is where everyone checks in to trade stories about their lives and their families, and checks out whether their new training plan has finally helped them move up in the pack. Some of my non-running friends might jump in, and walk if they have to, if the race is for a good cause or it's held at their favorite bar. If I'm at a small race in an area where I don't know anyone, it's a good way to meet people, especially if there's a post-race barbeque or a party at the local pub. A local 10K might really be 9.8K or 10.2K, but that's just one more thing for everyone to argue about afterwards.

Enormous races have a more energetic buzz. The size of the race indicates that it is an Event. All kinds of people from all over show up in their brightly colored running gear. It's a fair, and the race for the blue ribbon is the centerpiece.

A large race needs to be organized more carefully to ensure the masses stay safe and everyone has fun. If it's not, soon it will become a small race. Runners talk to each other about races, and if a race runs out of water or the course is badly marked, word-of-mouth will kill the race faster than a snowstorm.

If it's a longer race, like a marathon, there's more tension at the start. You can feel the focus of the runners on the test ahead of them. For rookie marathoners, it might be the first time they've ever tried to do anything that required an extended period of training. Veterans know that no matter how much they've trained, the race can still go horribly wrong. Everybody knows that they'll need some time to recover afterwards, so this is their one shot at the distance for a while.

Running in a race series is another way to see how you measure up to other local runners.

For example, in my area New England Runner Magazine organizes their Pub Series, a string of smaller races hosted by local bars. Battling for points towards the series championship adds another level to the competition. You have to be fast, committed for the length of the series, and you have to structure your training so you're ready to run each race well and still recover in time for the next challenge.

The Hocomock Swamp Rat's Grand Pricks series puts together challenging races over a two-year period to determine "New England's toughest runner". Rat runners get points according to their results, plus bonus points for things like finishing the tougher races or running naked.

The USATF-New England Grand Prix is a step up in competiveness. It's a yearly series where individuals and clubs compete in races ranging from a 5K to a marathon. Grand Prix races attract more of the people who make running a central part of their lives, whether or not they're fast in an absolute sense. At the starting line, runners wearing club singlets outnumber those wearing funny t-shirts. They are trying to be as fast as they can, for themselves and to help their team. It's still fun, but it's serious fun.

I usually think of myself as the first slow guy in any race. That means everyone who's ahead of me is a fast runner, while everyone who's behind me is also slow. Using this definition, 10-20% of the entrants in a typical Pub Series race might be fast. In a USATF race, the number of fast runners is more like 50%.

Some races aren't part of an official series, but still attract a high percentage of the dedicated runners in the area. The Boston area has a series of winter and early spring races that local runners traditionally use to get ready for the Boston Marathon. This Boston Prep series starts in January with a 16-mile race in Derry, NH. The races increase in length as the season progresses, ending with the Eastern States 20 Miler, a race that traverses the seacoast from Maine, through New

Hampshire, to Massachusetts.

This far into my book, it should come as no surprise to you that I have obsessive-compulsive tendencies. I always try to do things as efficiently as possible, especially when it's something I do repeatedly. For example, when I'm making coffee, I always start the beans grinding first, and while that's happening, I set the refrigerator to dispense 19 ounces of water into the coffee pot. Then I can put the filter in its holder, the ground beans into the filter, and the holder into the coffeemaker while the pot is filling. Pour the water into the coffee maker, turn it on, and coffee is on the way! The process gets me coffee in the minimum amount of time, and the routine keeps me from making stupid mistakes, even though I'm pre-coffee. It gives me a comfortable feeling knowing that I have a plan, even for something as simple as coffee.

When I'm running in an important race, especially if the race is the culmination of a long period of training, I tend to get a little wound up when the race finally arrives. So I have a pre-race routine that helps me control the anxiety and make preparing for the race, without ruining what I've built to get there, as simple as making coffee.

My final preparation for a race starts days before with a taper. I run slower and for less distance than I usually do, so I can make sure I'm rested for the race. Tapering off for a few days is enough for a 5K or a 10K. Longer races require longer tapers. I usually plan on a two-week taper for a marathon. Tapering sounds easy, but it's not. Slacking off leaves me with plenty of time to be anxious about whether I'm ready, or if I'm losing fitness, or if I'm gaining weight.

When I was younger, a day or two before the race I used to get an especially short "race haircut" to help me feel lighter, faster, and cooler (temperature-wise) than usual. Now that I'm in my 40s, my forehead has expanded into space formerly covered by hair, and my regular haircut has gotten shorter. Even though extra hair isn't the issue it used to be, I still head to the barber before a big race.

The day before a race I try to rest, but time seems to crawl if I spend it sitting around waiting for the next day to arrive. If I've traveled to a new place for the race, one way to pass time is to walk around and see some of the sights. It beats sitting around in a hotel room.

The night before the race, I try to eat food that's easily digestible, so by race time it will have completed working its way through my system. I often eat plenty of carbohydrates the day before a race. I've experimented, and as far as I can tell there's no need for carbo loading, even for longer races. As long as I eat a healthy, balanced diet, I'm fine. Still, I like pasta, and I'll be running off the extra calories the next day, so why not?

I make sure I have everything I need for race day. That includes clothing, running shoes, anti-chafing lube, proof of registration, and directions to the race. I toss a set of safety pins in the bag. I have plenty of them around from previous races. The race will usually supply pins, but if they don't have enough, I'll still be able to pin my number on. If it's cold, or if I know I'm not coming home right after the race, I'll also pack a bag with dry clothes I can change into after the race.

If there is a course map or a race packet with a description of the race, I'll go over that and plan how I'm going to run the race. In particular, I like to know where the big hills are and what the approach to the finish looks like. Elevation maps are particularly useful, though they can be intimidating if it's an exceptionally hilly race.

At the end of the day, I do what I can to get a good night's sleep. Sometimes that means taking a pill. Otherwise, anxiety about the next day can keep me awake. An over-the-counter antihistamine usually works well enough as long as I don't take them regularly.

On race day, it's important that I get up early enough to have time to unload the food I ate the day before. I also like to take a shower before a race, even though I'm just going out to get sweaty afterwards. A nice hot shower helps loosen up my muscles, and I just like starting out clean. It helps me feel better about myself going into the race.

I drink plenty of fluids before the race, but I don't eat anything on race morning unless the start of the race is later in the day or it's an exceptionally long race.

There are two things I always wear for a race. One is my Somerville Road Runners singlet, the other is a bright red jockstrap that I only use in races. When I put those on, I know it's time to compete. After that, I choose whatever running clothes are appropriate for the weather. On cold days, I wear less than I would on a regular running day because I know the extra effort of racing will make me warmer.

If I got my race number ahead of time, I pin it to my singlet before I leave. If there's a timing chip I put that on too. Then one last trip to the bathroom, and it's time to go.

I always make sure to leave early enough so that I arrive at the race at least an hour ahead of time. That way I have time to deal with registration, make another trip to the bathroom, and go out for a warm-up before the race begins.

In a 5K, there's no time to ease into race pace, so I'll often do another five kilometers beforehand as a warmup. I do most of my warmup at an easy jog, but I'll add some surges to try to find my good running form and lock into my race pace. If I have a course map, I'll run the entire course to warm up. Knowing where the hills are and when I'm close enough to the end to run all out is a big advantage.

The longer the race, the shorter and slower my warm up

gets. If it's a marathon, I might just swing my legs back and forth a few times to loosen them up before the start, and then run the first mile or two under my goal pace while I get warm.

When it's time to line up for the start, I try to find my proper place among the other running junkies, all nervously twitching in place like we're waiting for the man to bring us our fix. Too far back and I'll have to weave through all the slower runners ahead of me. Too far forward and I'll be discouraged when the faster runners who started behind me go by. Either one makes it more difficult for me to keep from going out too fast at the beginning of the race.

One time I saw a couple of women smoking cigarettes while they were waiting to start, which might have helped calm their nerves but still seemed somewhat counter-productive. I don't quite understand the people with iPods either. An iPod is great for keeping me company on a training run, but when I'm at a race, it's just a distraction that keeps me from focusing on my running or enjoying the company of my fellow runners.

While we wait, I'll chat with the other runners. We usually end up talking about the course and our goals for the day. I usually have multiple goals. There's a goal that I'll share with people, which is usually pretty realistic, and enough to keep me happy if I make it. Then there's a tougher goal that I keep to myself. It might be a little unlikely, but it's one that I think is within reach if everything goes well. Multiple goals are an effort to manage expectations, especially my own. The secret goal helps make the public goal seem more accessible, and that helps reduce my stress level.

Finally the gun sounds, and we're off. After all that waiting, I've got a lot of pent-up energy. If I'm not careful, I'll go out at an overly optimistic pace. That feels good in the initial rush at the start. But just when I start to dream that maybe this time, finally, I can hold onto my fast pace until the finish, my lungs and legs start to burn, my form goes to hell, and my speed dies. Other runners start going by, and the race turns into a painful survival-fest.

Going out too fast isn't the worst thing that can happen in a race. Getting hurt is worse. Losing five minutes in a 5-mile race while waiting for a train to finish crossing the course happened to me once, and that was frustrating too. But going out too fast is the most common way I screw up a race. It happens a lot more often than I'd like, especially if I've been focusing my training on a specific race. You think I'd learn....

My best races have often been ones where I was ready to run well, but I didn't feel a need to show it that particular day. Then I start out at a comfortable pace and when the race gets hard later on, I still have something left for a strong finish. My first Boston Marathon was like that. I was just running to enjoy the experience, and I ended up with what was by far my best time at Boston.

My enthusiasm also gets the better of me sometimes when I'm running downhill. I'm better off if I dial it back and maintain good form, but it's hard to keep from using the hill to go as fast as possible. That pays off in the short term, but leaves me worn down from the pounding when I'm looking for the energy to finish the race.

On the other hand, I usually walk through water stops. It's slower, but I've never been really good at drinking on the run, so I walk a little instead. It's easier to drink if I fold the top of the cup together. Folding the cup keeps the drink from sloshing out and lets me draw it through the narrow opening instead of trying to pour it into my mouth, but unfortunately a lot of races use plastic cups that crack when I fold them.

If it's a short race and it's hot, I'll dump the water on my head to cool off instead of drinking. If I do that, it's important to ensure that the cup holds water, and not a sugary sports drink.

The water usually sits out for a while before I get to it, getting lukewarm and collecting bugs and dirt. You have to take your chances. The water at one race near Lake Champlain tasted like it came directly from the lake. It crawled around in my stomach until I finally lost the struggle to keep it down in the home stretch. I still might have held on for an age group prize, but unfortunately, it took two vomit breaks before I could get all the water out of my system.

The first two-thirds of any race are always a balancing act, no matter what the distance. Whether it's the first two miles of a 5K or the first 18 miles of a marathon, the finish line seems like it will never arrive. I'm trying to go as fast as I can without going too fast or letting my form get sloppy. I'm never quite sure whether I should turn it up one last notch, or whether pushing just that little bit more will ruin my race. Unless I've already gone too fast and fallen apart, there's always room to go a little faster.

Then I get to the last third of the race, and my whole attitude changes. I can feel the finish line start to call me. It may get hard – if I've set my pace correctly, it *will* get hard -- but I only need to hold on and keep doing what I'm doing all the way to the finish.

My mind gets lost in what I'm doing. Maybe there's pain, and maybe the last step was hard, but I know that I made it through that step, and the next one probably won't be any worse. Soon enough, another pain shows up to distract me from the old pain, and I accept that too. All I have to do is keep taking the next step. If I do, the finish will arrive, almost by itself.

When the finish line comes into view, it's time to see what's left in the tank. If I've run slowly, I might not think it's worth kicking in to squeeze out a second or two. Too fast, and

I don't have the choice. I can't go any faster. But if I've run a good race, I've got a little extra left, just enough to sprint to the finish. I might not make it much past the finish line before I have to stop catch my breath, and sometimes throw up, but that's OK.

My race routine isn't compulsive, really. Really! I've gotten to the point where I don't have to test how hard I can go in *every* race. I can treat some races just like any other run. I get up, dress and go out for some fun. The biggest differences between these races and a typical run are that I have to pay an entry fee and there are many more people running with me than usual. Then, my enjoyment comes from hanging around with other people who share my love of running. As I've gotten older (and slower) this reason to race has become more important.

When I'm running to socialize, I'll start slow, then ease into my race pace. By running the race at a pace that allows me to talk, I can meet lots of interesting people. We'll have at least one thing in common to talk about, and as we converse we're likely to find others. If we don't, the natural flow of the race will separate us, and I can move on to other people.

By starting slow, I'm often the better runner in the conversation. That's an advantage when I'm trying to run and talk. Not everyone wants to talk, especially people who are running as fast as they can while I'm lounging along. But I can still help some of those people, by serving as a distraction or a pacer or an advisor.

Once the race is over, it's time to celebrate, commiserate, and refuel with the other runners. A good race has finish areas where there's space for the runners to hang out, food, water, beer and other drinks, bathrooms, and shelter in case the weather's bad. It's an extra bonus if there are free massages or showers to help me relax and recover.

After the excitement is over, I need to recover from my effort. That keeps me from jumping right back into hard training. Sometimes, if the race was the focus of a long period of training, it can be hard to find another goal to get me going again. But even when my enthusiasm wanes, habit keeps me going through the motions. Then something new appears, as it always does, and it's time to start planning for the next race.

The most dangerous thing for me is a successful race. Since I enjoy racing as much as I do, when it's going well I just want to keep racing. But then I race too often, without allowing enough recovery between races, and it's just like training too hard. Soon, my results start to fall off, and if I keep pushing to try and get back where I was, I get sick or injured. But I'm learning – I think.

My first marathon – Vermont City in 1993

Chapter 7: The Long Road to the Marathon

"My training could best be described as binge and splurge. I allowed life to get in the way, and hadn't caught the bug enough to push through winter training. I would re-start each spring, and of course, I found it difficult again.

Fast forward 10 or so years. I started the year with a group of others doing a "Couch to 5K" program that got me out 3 days per week. The bogeyman winter was around the corner, so I signed up for a spring marathon, and used that as motivation to continue running all winter, mostly outside, and I got up to distances I had never seen before."
-Mark Bates

In 1972, McDonalds gave away game pieces for a contest. Each piece had a different Olympic event printed inside. If the US won a medal in the event shown on your game piece, you won a prize. Frank Shorter won the gold medal in the marathon that year. I won a Big Mac, and I also gained an ongoing interest in marathons.

So when I started entering road races in 1992, I already had marathon running in the back of my mind. Shorter races were fine, a good way to get together with my friends and work up a thirst. But I didn't spend much time trying to get my 5 or 10K times down before I started working on a marathon. My first race was a local 4-mile run in June. I built up to a long run of 11 miles, and then ran a half-marathon in October of that year. Those 13 miles were the furthest I had ever run. After I survived that, I signed up for the Vermont City Marathon, scheduled for Memorial Day weekend in May of 1993.

I kept building up my mileage. On January 3, 1993, I extended my long run up to 15-1/2 miles. I thought I was doing well, with plenty of time to get ready for the race in May. The following weekend, I developed a pain in the outside of my right knee during a 9-mile run. When I stopped running, the pain subsided. It wasn't that bad during day-to-day activities, but every time I tried to run, the pain would flare up after a mile or two. I wanted to keep training, so I got into a cycle where I'd rest for a day or two, my knee would feel better, and I'd give it another try. The pain would start up again, limiting me to a short run. This went on for a couple of weeks.

Finally, I gave up and I stopped running for an entire month. The only exercise I got during that time was from "running" in a pool with a flotation belt strapped around my waist to hold me up. I also got a podiatrist to make me a set of orthotics, shoe inserts intended to provide support to accommodate some of the imperfections in my body and smooth out my stride.

At the end of February I was able to ease back into running. By the time my marathon arrived, I'd built back up to a long run of 15 miles. I didn't think I was ready to run the entire marathon, but Vermont City has a marathon relay in addition to the marathon. I found two other people on the Internet, and we put together a relay team so I wouldn't have to run the whole thing myself.

When I got to race registration to pick up our relay numbers, I wandered over to the marathon registration area and checked, and my number was there. I already had paid for it, so I figured I might as well pick it up too. There was no sense in letting it go to waste.

The Vermont City Marathon starts and finishes near Battery Park in downtown Burlington. The course loops back through the park a couple of times and most of the relay exchange points are there. Spectators can stay near the park and see their friends at multiple points in the race without having to move far.

I was running the first 10 miles of the race for my relay team. The morning of the race, I decided to pin my marathon number on under my relay number before I headed to the start. I figured I'd start the race, and while I was running, I'd figure out whether I wanted to keep going after I passed the relay baton on to my teammate. There wasn't much risk. Because of the loops in the course, even if dropped out before the finish, I wouldn't be too far from the park and my friends.

It was a beautiful day to run and the enthusiasm of the runners and the crowd in Battery Park was contagious. I felt great after completing my 10-mile portion of the relay, so I took off my relay number and kept going. By mile 14, I fell in with a group running at my pace and we traveled along the shore of Lake Champlain telling jokes and having a fine time. The hill from the lake up to Battery Park at mile 17 was tough, but the beat from the Taiko drummers stationed there carried us up the hill to the crowd cheering in the park.

Unfortunately, by the time I got to mile 21, the fun was over. When I turned onto the bike path along the lakeshore for the last 5 miles, I was tired, sore, and sweaty and I had to slow to a walk. But having come this far, I was determined to finish. Quitting was not an option. Nothing was going to get in my way. I walked half of the final 5 miles, and I had to talk a medical aid worker out of pulling me off the course, but I made it to the finish line with a final time of 4:02:19.

The race left me wanting more. It had been an enormous effort, but I was proud of my accomplishment when I finally finished, and I loved the camaraderie among the runners as we all worked towards the same goal. I wanted to try again, and this time, get it right.

But first, I had to recover from the race. I was used to being tired after a long run, and I was even more tired and sore after getting through 26 miles. What I didn't know was that it would get worse. When I woke up the next day, I was so sore I could barely walk. It's called "Delayed Onset Muscle Soreness". Going down stairs was especially hard. It was easier to go down backwards. The pain was even worse the next day. On the third day, I finally began to feel a little better.

The pain went away, leaving behind my determination to improve. I decided to try Vermont City again the next year. I knew I had to prepare better if I wanted better results. This time around, with the help of my orthotics, I remained injury-free, and I got my long run up to 23 miles before the race. Race day was warm, but I ran well until calf cramps slowed me to a crawl for the last couple of miles. I brought my time down to 3:31, but I still wasn't satisfied.

The 100th Boston Marathon was coming up in 1996. It promised to be a major event, and I wanted to be part of it. I signed up for the Baystate Marathon in 1995, figuring I could use the notoriously flat and fast course to qualify for the 100th Boston Marathon in 1996. I was 34, so I needed a 3:10 to qualify. That was much faster than my previous marathons, but I thought that if I could manage to run the entire distance, my times in shorter races indicated that the goal was possible. I trained even harder, but unfortunately I was sick the week before the race, and I found I just didn't have the endurance on race day. I ran the whole race this time, but I was only slightly faster than before, finishing in 3:29. I ended up watching the 100th Boston from the side of the road, quietly seething with frustration that I wasn't out there running myself.

I didn't run another marathon until 1999, when I ran Vermont City again. Vermont in May can be comfortably cool, but on this day the temperatures reached the mid-80s. I crashed and burned in the heat, shuffling slowly from mile 17 until about mile 23. Then I got a cup of icewater from a little girl who was next to the bike path, watching the race. I drained the cup, and that refreshed me enough so I could pick it up and run to the end. I finished in 3:55.

By 2000, I had reached the point where what I wanted most out of running was to qualify for the Boston Marathon. Boston is one of the most famous sporting events in the world, and it's held every spring, virtually in my own back yard. I was never going to get into the World Series or the Super Bowl, but I could still have 150,000 people cheering for me as I ran the same race with some of the best runners in the world.

I could get into Boston by collecting money for a charity or by getting a number from my running club, but I wanted to qualify. I was never going to be a champion runner, but at least I could earn my way into one of running's signature events.

My marathon times had improved some, but I had never gotten within 15 minutes of qualifying. Luckily, I was getting older. That took no effort at all. When I turned 40, my qualifying time for Boston would rise to three hours and 20 minutes, 10 minutes slower than the time for the open division. That was much closer to the times I had been running, though I still had about 10 minutes to make up somehow. So in 2000, I made a conscious decision to dial back my other running and take a more focused, long-term approach to qualifying for the marathon.

I never really had felt good about my pacing in any of my marathons. I was finishing, but I never ran strongly the whole way. The 3:20 marathon I needed to qualify for Boston would require holding a pace of about 7:38 per mile. I knew from my times in shorter races that I had plenty of speed. What I lacked was the endurance to hold that speed to the end of the marathon.

I turned 40 in the summer of 2001, so 2002 would be the first Boston where I could take advantage of the 3:20 qualifying time. I decided to aim towards a qualifying marathon in the fall of 2001, when it's cooled off some after a summer of training through the heat. I figured that would be easier than running a marathon in warm spring weather after training through the cold New England winter. A fall 2001 race gave me about a year and a half to prepare.

The key to building the endurance I needed for a marathon is the long run. In the past I had followed a standard training plan, which called for a long run every two weeks starting at 10 miles or so, and increasing a couple miles every time, topping out in the low 20s three weeks before the race. That wasn't working out so well. It left me trying to run both farther and faster on race day. I was also doing my hardest long runs just before the race, so I wasn't always as fresh going into the race as I would like.

This time around, I was going to take more time to increase the length of my long run. If I built up slower, I figured I wouldn't be as worn down when race day arrived. I was also going to try to run more than 26 miles while training, and still leave time to drop my long run back down below 26 miles before the race.

I continued to do a long run every two weeks, but I only increased the mileage on every other long run. Then the next week, I cut back on my mileage to ensure that I got enough rest to recover completely before I returned to my regular routine.

The other big change I made was to keep my eyes on the goal, and give somewhat less than my best effort when I entered other races. I still ran in shorter races to socialize with my friends and have fun, but I treated them like fast training runs instead of all-out races. That saved more of my energy for marathon training.

Running the races leading up to my goal marathon at less than full effort was also part of my mental training for the marathon. The worst thing anyone can do in a marathon is go out too fast. Inevitably, you'll crash and burn and struggle to finish. Knowing ahead of time that I wasn't going to run the race all-out helped me to learn to manage my excitement at the start of races so I could pace myself better.

When I raced, I stuck to my training plan, and even though I wasn't trying as hard as I possibly could, I found that I was still getting faster. This reinforced the idea that I was doing the right thing.

When my long runs got longer, I started taking three weeks between them. That allowed even more recovery time to get ready for the next one.

I decided that the Hartford Marathon in October 2001 would be my target race. Hartford was near home. The course was flat for the first 20 miles, so it would be easier to get to that point and still have energy for the finish. There were typically fewer than 2000 entrants, so the race wouldn't be too crowded, but there would still be enough runners at or near my pace so I'd always have somebody to run with. There were even pace groups. Someone would be running the race, leading people who were trying to finish at 3:20. I could run with that group if I needed them to help me meet my goal.

At the end of May, I ran Vermont City again. This time I ran it as a training run. I finished in 3:41, and at that pace I had enough endurance so I didn't suffer from excessive soreness after the race.

In the summer, I sweated through another 26-mile run followed by two 28-mile runs. Then I scaled back to 22- and

20-mile runs in September before I started to taper down for the race.

Tapering is always a mixed blessing. It's great to finish the hardest part of my training for a marathon, take it easy, and relax. In theory it is, anyhow. In practice, when I start to run less, I worry about losing my fitness, I worry about gaining weight, and I have extra time on my hands to worry about whether I'm ready to run the race.

The day before the race, I headed to Hartford. I could have driven down on the morning of the race, but I wanted to check into a hotel and have the evening to relax and prepare for the marathon. Unfortunately, by this time I was just too wound up. I'd been working towards this race for a year and a half, and trying to qualify for Boston for years before that. Resting would have been the best thing to do, but I just couldn't do it. Instead, I spent a couple hours walking around, trying to find something interesting to distract me from worrying about the next day's race. The search failed, and I ended up back in the hotel room, watching a movie and getting my gear ready for the morning.

My plan for the race was to ease into the race and run the first two miles slower than my goal pace in order to keep from going out too fast. I wanted to run at an 8:30 pace to start. I'd have to run a little faster than the required average of 7:38 for the remaining 24 miles, but not too much faster. A conservative start would hopefully pay off in the end.

I wrote all the splits I was aiming for upside down on my race number. That way I could track my progress without the need to do the math in my head when I got tired. Then I went to bed, tossing and turning through the night, waiting for it to be time to get up and run.

The next day, the weather at the start was sunny and in the 50's, fine weather for running. I lined up back in the pack with the slower runners, but when the gun went off, it was still hard to keep from racing out with everyone else. I caught up with Steve Pepe, another Somerville Road Runner, and we chatted as we ran together, which helped keep me on track. I have a picture of the start, and you can see from the clear space in front of Steve and I that we're running easily and letting people go by.

A mile into the race, I left Steve and eased into my race pace. The first 19 miles of the race was out and back along the Connecticut River. It was very flat but not very scenic. I ran well, keeping just a little ahead of my goal pace through each mile. A little before mile 20 I finished making up the time I lost at the beginning of the race and I passed the 3:20 pace group. I knew that I just had to stay ahead of them and I would qualify for Boston.

Passing the pace group energized me, just when I might have been hitting the wall if things weren't going well. I left the pace group behind as the course passed by the start and took off for the final six-mile loop. I was getting tired, and there were more hills on the section, but by this point I could smell the finish line. I held my pace to the end, and I finished a little over 3:17, which was a PR by 12 minutes. I was going to Boston!

The 2002 Boston Marathon was my reward for all my hard work. I planned on taking it easy in the race and enjoying the event. I scaled back my training, topping out at a long run of 20 miles. My taper was only two weeks instead of the three weeks that everyone recommends. SRR rented a bus to take the runners from the club to the start, so I didn't have to get up at dawn, ride a school bus out with all the other runners, and hang out in a field for hours waiting for the race to begin. I showed up at the starting line feeling good, relaxed and just happy to be there.

The weather was just about perfect when the gun went off, overcast and in the 50s. The excitement and the energy from the massive crowd carried me along. I barely paid attention to how I was doing for about 17 miles. I reached the hills in Newton and kept right on running. I slowed a little as I climbed, but I had no trouble getting through them.

At the top of Heartbreak Hill I had a little over 6 miles to go and I realized that I had run much faster than I had expected and I still felt good. I knew that the rest of the course was mostly flat, trending slightly downhill. So I decided to pick up the pace and see what would happen. I had averaged something over 7:20 per mile until then. For the last 10K, I brought that down to a little under 7:10. I crossed the finish in front of the cheering crowds on Boylston St. in just over 3:14, three minutes faster than I ran Hartford, on a harder course with less training.

I ran a 3:13 that fall at Cape Cod, but all things considered, Boston 2002 was probably my most successful marathon. I've run Boston three times since then and none have gone as well. 2004 was a particular disappointment. I trained hard and well, and I was getting results that indicated I was ready to run a fast marathon. Then on race day temperatures reached 85, making it one of the hottest Boston Marathons on record. A fast time was impossible. I ended up getting a bag and some ice from a spectator and attaching it to my head to keep cool while I trotted to the finish in 3:46.

A marathon allows my OCD tendencies to reach full flower. A lot of pieces have to come together in order to run a fast marathon. Some of them are beyond my control, so it's important to my mental well-being to identify the ones I can control and have a plan to take care of them.

First and most importantly, I have to get my training in. For me, the most important part of training for a marathon is building the endurance. There's no substitute for building up my long run to 26 miles or more, with enough total miles in the bank and plenty of recovery time so those long runs don't leave me totally drained afterwards.

Running race distance or more gets me used to passing through the "wall". The wall is real. Somewhere around 17 to 21 miles, everyone runs low on carbohydrates and starts to use fat more to fuel their running. That's not an easy transition, but I found that if I practiced it, I got accustomed to running through the wall without slowing down.

Most training plans have you increasing your long run every time, peaking with your last run before the race. I prefer to leave enough time after my longest run to do a few, shorter long runs leading to the race. If I build up to 26-28 miles first, then two 20-mile runs afterwards seem relatively easy, and they still add to my preparation for the race.

I do a little speedwork, but no more than 10% of my total mileage. Most of the time, the races I enter for fun are more than enough. When I'm training fast, I try to focus more on running efficiently instead of running as fast as I possibly can.

If I'm really interested in a fast time, I have to pick a fast course. There are other considerations, like the difficulty of travel to the race and whether I can find a convenient place to stay, but if I want to run fast, I need to find a fairly flat course. Not dead flat. There should be some gentle hills so I'm not using the same muscles the same way for the entire race. An overall drop in elevation from start to finish is good, but any steep up- (or down-) hills can counteract that advantage. For example, the Boston Marathon finish is about 450 lower than the start, but the hills along the way keep it from being a particularly fast course.

I make sure I know what sports drink will be available at the water stops during the race. If I'm not familiar with the drink, I'll try it out while I train so I know I can tolerate it on race day. I learned this the hard way in my first marathon, when the sports drink they were using gave me stomach cramps. Most races provide water as an alternative, but in a marathon, I want the additional carbohydrates and electrolytes found in the sports drink.

I have to be well-rested on race day. It's important to train carefully, and allow enough recovery while I'm building my endurance so my training builds me up instead of grinding me down. My pre-race taper won't be enough recovery time if I've been overdoing it in training for months beforehand. I find that when I train properly, a two-week taper is more than enough rest to get me ready for the race. Many training plans recommend a three-week taper, but as long as I haven't done too much beforehand, that third week is just an extra week of counterproductive anxious waiting.

I need to eat properly to perform well. Doritos and beer are tasty, but real food makes for better fuel. When I cut down on the sugary or fried foods I do better, but the call of the bacon-cheeseburger and ice cream is hard to ignore. Whatever I'm eating, if I'm running well on that diet before the race, there's no benefit in changing my eating habits as the race approaches. The day before the race is the only day I might adjust my meal choices. I'll eat more carbohydrates, usually pasta, to store up a little more easily accessible energy. More importantly, I avoid foods that are hard for me to digest, like steak. I've had some good races after eating fettuccine alfredo with some chicken and broccoli, so that's become my lucky pre-race meal.

I try to prepare as much as I can the day before the race, so I have as little as possible to worry about on race day. If I'm running a course that's new to me and there's time, I'll drive the course to get a better look at how difficult it's going to be.

That night I'll get all my clothes out, pin my number on my shirt, and make sure I have my energy gels ready to go. I'll write my goal pace chart on my number, upside down so I can read it easily while running. Writing down the splits for every five miles is enough to keep me on track, and allows enough space to let the uphill and downhill miles balance out. Finally, I'll put out the pre-race snacks and drinks I'll want the next morning.

Then it's time to relax and get some sleep. I'm still working on that part. I have learned that if I've been getting enough sleep on the nights leading up to the race, it's not a big problem if I don't sleep well the night before the race.

On race morning all I need to do is get up early enough to ensure I have time to eat a little, hydrate a lot, make any last-minute weather-related clothing and gear choices, and go to the bathroom. Then it's time to head to the start and run.

When the race starts, I try to start slow and use the first mile or two as a warm up. There's a long way to go, and I'll need all the energy I can muster later on. The beginning of the race should be easy. If I'm struggling at all before 16 miles, it's not my day.

During the race, I drink whenever I can to minimize dehydration. The only time I'll skip a water stop is towards the end of the race, when there isn't enough time left to absorb any more fluid. Often by then I can feel the drinks I've already had still sloshing around in my stomach.

I like to have an energy gel every five miles during the race. That allows me to stretch out my carbohydrate stores further before I run out and hit the wall. By taking the gels regularly, I keep my blood sugar level up and avoid sugar rushes and crashes. I've learned to carry the gels in a neoprene waist pack. The first time I ran a race with gels, I carried them in a pocket in my shorts designed to hold sunglasses. The gels swung back and forth as I ran, rubbing against my leg to create an uncomfortable raw spot. The next race, I tried shorts that had mesh pockets designed to carry gels. My gel packets fell out within 100 yards of the start. I couldn't stop to pick them up without getting in everyone's way, and the pack of runners quickly trampled the gels into the street.

I carry ibuprophen to battle pain and inflammation during the race. If NSAIDs (nonsteroidal anti-inflammatory drugs) bother your stomach, you can use acetaminophen instead. It helps with the pain but doesn't do anything for inflammation.

Unfortunately, no matter how well I prepare things can go wrong. A marathon is too hard. There's no way anyone can guarantee that they'll be able to handle every possible adversity. No one can say with certainty how they will do. Sometimes you just have a bad day. Maybe you weren't rested enough, maybe you picked up a cold, or maybe you just don't feel right, and it shows in your time. Sometimes pain gets in the way, whether it's something as simple as a bad blister or it's a more debilitating injury, like a cramp or a torn calf muscle. And sometimes the weather turns on you. Maybe there's a 20 mph wind blowing a cold rain in your face, or maybe it's 85 and sunny and the spectators are comfortable wearing less than the runners. When trouble strikes, do what you can, but remember that there's always another race.

Like most runners, I'm a goal-oriented person. An objective helps keep me going. I wouldn't put in the effort necessary to run a marathon if I didn't enjoy the pride I feel when I reach my target. My first marathon goal was typical for many people. I just wanted to make it to the finish. Once I did that, my next goal was to try to finish faster.

For some people, their goal is to accumulate marathon finishes. So many people have run marathons in all 50 states or on all seven continents that they've formed a club.

SRR members Steve Pepe and Kevin Counihan have run together for years. They reached their goal of finishing their 100th marathon at Boston in 2010 and have started working on their second hundred. Steve's marathon PR is a little over 3 hours, but now he runs races in over 5 hours with Kevin, whose right foot was severely injured in a lawn mower accident when he was 4.

Some runners combine speed and quantity goals. Gary Allen, the race director of the MDI Marathon, reached his goal of completing his 50th sub-3 hour marathon before his 50th birthday. He's also one of a limited number of runners who have run sub-3 in five different decades, and he's made a bet that he'll add his sixth decade in 2020.

As I write this, I've completed 18 marathons. As I get older, it gets harder to match the times I've run in the past, let alone go even faster. I keep running marathons, but the reasons I run them have changed. These days, I like running races in new places. I get to see 26 miles of new territory, meet some new people, do a long run without the need to carry my own sports drinks, and I often find a celebration when I finish. An ideal course is interesting to run, not necessarily flat and fast. It may go through a new city, or pass through exceptionally scenic natural settings. I still like to challenge myself to run fast, but comfort is important too. The race should be well organized, and a hotel room near the start is ideal (though plenty of bushes can suffice).

For example, in early May of 2008, Ruth and I went out to California for the Avenue of the Giants Marathon. The race was on a Sunday in the Humboldt Redwood State Park, about 250 miles north of San Francisco, along with a half-marathon and a 10K. My goal was to run comfortably, finish under 4 hours, stay injury-free, and leave something in the tank for another Vermont City run on Memorial Day weekend. Ruth wanted to improve on her 2:06+ from her first half-marathon in February.

The quickest way from the San Francisco airport to the race is to take US Route 101, a major highway that takes you straight to the race start. We didn't want to do both a six-hour flight and a boring five-hour drive on the day before the race, especially as Ruth would be doing all the driving. So Ruth and I flew into San Francisco the Friday before and we broke up the trip with a stop to spend the night along the way.

Instead of pulling off 101 somewhere, we decided to stay on the Pacific coast in Mendocino. The trip from 101 to the coast took us along CA Route 128, a narrow, winding road through the hills of Mendocino County wine country. There were many twists that Ruth needed to navigate carefully, but plenty of scenery to look as we wound our way through.

The hills continued right to the shore. We didn't see ocean until we made one last turn, Rt.128 suddenly ended, and the coast appeared. We turned and took the coastal highway (CA1) north and enjoyed dramatic views of the ocean as we drove into Mendocino.

In Mendocino, we stayed at the Blackberry Inn, a very nice place on the landward side of the coastal highway with a view of the ocean. Mendocino is a small, touristy town, with nice restaurants, galleries, and the like. In the summer it's a busy seaside getaway, but in May it's pleasantly quiet.

I don't usually run the day before a marathon, but I couldn't resist the three miles or so of trail along the cliffs that surround the town and overlook the ocean. They made for a stunningly beautiful 5-mile run on Saturday morning from the inn, around the town, and back. Between multiple stops to ooh and aah at the scenery and running carefully to avoid tripping and falling over the edge of the cliffs, I didn't work too hard.

After some browsing and lunch in town, we headed north along CA1. Again, the views were stunning. Then CA1 turned back east into the mountains. The winding roads we were traveling on before were nothing compared to the next stretch. Ruth didn't get a minute to relax for more than 50 miles, while I kept a tight grip on the Jesus handle over the passenger-side window as we twisted up, down, and through. The views were tremendous, as long as you didn't think too much about the possibility of driving off a cliff.

We finally made it to Redway, where we stayed the night before the race in a cabin at the Dean Creek Resort. Sunday morning we packed up and headed 20 miles up 101 to the start.

The race starts under a 101 overpass at the intersection of Bull Creek Road and the Avenue of the Giants at exit 663. Since that exit was blocked off for the race, runners were directed to leave the highway at the next exit to the north and drive back to the start. There was ample parking on a dry wash next to the Eel River, but access to the parking from the road was slow. People who didn't heed the warning to get there at least an hour early were stuck in the line of cars waiting to park. Many of those people missed the start of the race, though with chip timing that wasn't a disaster.

The marathon course goes out to the west and back along Bull Creek Road, then takes a 90-degree right turn and goes out to the south and back along the Avenue of the Giants. The course is very runnable. The first half rolls a little, trending up on the way out and down coming back. The road is a little rough, but not too bad. The second half felt like a nice easy downhill going out, but it wasn't much of a downhill, because it felt flat on the way back. The only real hill is a bridge over 101 that's a downhill at mile 14 and an uphill coming back at mile 25. The hill is nothing major, but the climb comes at a difficult point in the race if you're running on fumes. They use the same course for the Humboldt Marathon in the fall, with the first and second halves reversed.

The half-marathoners start with the marathoners and run the Bull Creek Road portion. The 10K starts a half-hour after the other races and goes out and back on the Avenue of the Giants, out of the way of the longer races.

The day was just about perfect. It was in the 50s and overcast. Even if it had been sunny, the redwoods would have kept us in the shade for most of the course. There was some wind, but the trees shielded us from most of it.

I ran the first mile or so with Ruth. We hit the first mile marker at 12 minutes, which was slower than we'd planned, and then I pulled away. I made it to mile 2 at 18 minutes, so I didn't take the first split too seriously. Mile markers the rest of the way seemed accurate enough.

The trees were majestic. Their commanding presence and dignity added an unusual aura to the event, meeting every expectation we had when we decided to travel across the country for the race. Every once in a while, I'd tilt my head back and follow a particularly imposing tree as it reached to the sky, but that made it hard to hold to a straight line while I was running, so for the most part I kept my head down and just moved my eyes to take in the sights.

Since I started slowly, once I hit my pace I was passing people for most of the race. On an out and back course, the first people you see coming back are usually the leaders. Here, the Avenue of the Giants lets slower runners start an hour early to get everyone out of the way so they can reopen the roads sooner. That meant the first people coming back were some of the early birds. The competitor in me didn't like seeing all those slow runners ahead of me.

When I finally saw a fast runner, he was wearing a Greater Boston singlet. I was in a race all the way across the country, and I still wasn't the fastest runner from Massachusetts in the field.

I hit the first turnaround in just under an hour. On the way back, I stopped for five minutes around mile 9 at a port-a-potty. That was almost the only time anyone passed me the rest of the way.

About 350 people started the marathon, but between my slow start, the half-marathoners, a large number of relatively slow Team in Training runners, and all those early bird runners, the first half was more crowded than typical for a race of this size. Luckily, I left most of that behind at the turn onto the Avenue of the Giants. The second half of the marathon was a pleasant cruise among the trees on a much smoother road.

On the way south, I caught up with an older guy who was working on his seventh Avenue and we talked for a few miles. He told me he had developed the habit of counting the runners he saw coming back after the final turn so he'd know where he was in the field. I pulled ahead of him as we approached the turn, then when I saw him after I'd started on the way back, he told me that I was right at 100th place.

About mile 20, someone around my age passed by. It was the first time I'd been passed since the port-a-potty stop. I passed him back when he stopped at the next water station, then spent the next half-mile or so waiting for him to catch me again. When he finally did, I struck up another conversation and learned that Sam was working on his first marathon. He had done lots of cross training (telemark skiing, etc...), but his longest run before the marathon was only 13 miles, so he was struggling a bit. I paced him through mile 25, which also helped me go a little faster than I would have otherwise, so we both ate up a number of other runners. Then, once we made it over the hill at mile 25, he got excited about reaching the finish and he raced in. I sped up some too, but realized that I'd have to strain to keep up with Sam. I had Vermont in three weeks, so I let him go.

At the finish, we got our medals and I found Ruth. It turns out that Sam was one of the people who had gotten a late start, so his chip time was actually about 10 minutes faster than mine. Since he was 48 that meant he'd qualified for Boston on his first attempt. That meant more to me than it did to Sam, who was looking at the marathon as a once in a lifetime lark, inspired by a friend who'd been training hard after having a miserable time in his own first marathon.

Ruth and I both had good days. Ruth set a half-marathon PR by over 6 minutes, finishing 9th in her age group in 2:00:27. I ended up finishing comfortably in 3:45, 5th in my age group and 66th out of 347 overall. I was tired, but I thought I'd be able to recover fast enough to run Vermont on Memorial Day weekend.

Sam turned back to jog out and wait for a friend. Ruth and I got in the car and headed back to Mendocino, since we'd figured a five-hour drive after a race wouldn't be much fun either. On Monday we got up, went on a kayak tour along the shore, then drove to San Francisco. We stayed the rest of the week in the Flower Child Room in the Red Victorian B&B in Haight-Ashbury.

Post-race, I was ready for my normal run on Tuesday. I did 8 miles in Golden Gate Park after a hard day of tourism (Coit Tower, Fisherman's Wharf, and cable cars). I was a little sore, but it was nothing compared to how I usually felt after racing a marathon.

Saturday morning, after an excellent week of touristing, Ruth and I headed back to the airport for our flight home.

Three weeks later it was time for the 2008 Vermont City Marathon. I signed up for Vermont partly to support my friend

Mark, who was running his first marathon, and partly for the challenge of running two marathons in a single month.

We stayed at the Burlington Hilton, which is less than a quarter-mile from the start, making it the most convenient race headquarters around. By now I was an experienced runner, and I'd already run Vermont six times, so I was pretty relaxed before the race. I stopped by the expo and had some time to chat with a high school classmate, Tim Ritchie, whose National Running Center store has a big booth at VT.

The next day was hot and sunny, and I was reminded that no matter how many marathons I've run, there's always something more that the marathon can teach me. Humility is on the top of the list, and this race had others:

- When there isn't a cloud in the sky, wear sunscreen, especially on a course like Vermont where there's little shade.

- Pack sunscreen.

- Don't make fun of someone who wears a white, long sleeved wicking shirt on a sunny day when you're wearing a black singlet with no sunscreen.

- My white sun hat with the neck shade does me no good when I leave it at home. Brown hair does not reflect heat.

- Blisters on my feet often feel better after they break.

- Water is easier to manage than Gatorade, so it spends less time in the sun at aid stations.

- Hot Gatorade sucks.

- Counting cadence while I run helps keep me going forward when the little voice in my mind is telling me to take it easy.

- Sometimes the little voice is right.

- If I overdo it during a race in the heat and I'm dizzy and short of breath while standing around afterwards, it's a good idea to lie down.

- On a sunny day, it's dumb to lie down on the reflective blanket they give you at the finish.

While I've continued to run marathons, I haven't qualified for Boston lately. The last time I tried was at the Marine Corps Marathon in 2007. The MCM is the largest race I've ever run, with over 30,000 entrants. I stayed on track for a qualifying time while I ran past all the famous Washington, D.C. monuments, but around mile 20, while I was crossing the Potomac to leave the capitol, my calves cramped and I crashed. I trotted through the last six miles at about an 11-minute pace, watching sadly as streams of other runners passed me by.

Earlier in 2007, when I met Gary Allen in Maine, he mentioned that he travels to Boston each year to visit relatives for New Year's. Every New Year's morning, he gets up early and runs the Boston Marathon course. I decided to join him for the 2009 run along with three other people. Ned Swain came down from Portland just to run, and fellow SRR member Brandon Villarreal came over from nearby Maynard, MA.

Ruth, wonderful as always, got up at 4AM to give me a ride from our home in Arlington to the starting line in Hopkinton. Brandon had to get someone to cover the last three hours of his shift as a Maynard police officer, but he made it to the start at 6AM as scheduled. But there was no Gary. We waited 10 minutes, and then decided that we would do the run by ourselves. Brandon went off to park his car, but while Ruth and I were waiting for him to return Gary and Ned arrived. Gary had missed the exit from the Mass Pike, so he had to drive to the next exit, turn around, and head back.

So about 15-20 minutes late, with the sky just beginning to lighten a little in the east, we took off. It was frigid, about 3 degrees, and windy. Luckily, for the most part the wind came from behind us. Every once in a while the wind changed direction and reminded us that things could be much worse.

Soon the sun came up, and we settled into the run. The roads were in pretty good shape in spite of the previous day's snow. For the first few miles, while most people were still in bed recovering from their New Year's celebrations, the roads were essentially clear of cars. Gary insisted on following the actual marathon course, so from time to time we'd weave back and forth, following the tangents. At about 10 miles, he noticed that he'd accidentally turned off his watch, and no one else had bothered to mark the time we started. We decided that a starting time estimate of 6:20AM would be close enough.

We passed the time the way runners usually do on long runs, by sweating (with the sweat freezing upon contact with the air) and talking about running. Gary was the fastest runner, and he had stories for every section of the course, so he did a lot of the talking. I dragged out some of my old warhorses for a new audience.

Just after the halfway point was the section Gary rated as the toughest part of the race, the section between Wellesley College and the Newton hills. It's not as challenging to run as some of the other sections, but it comes after the burst of energy you get from the screaming coeds has worn off, and when you're looking forward to the Newton hills, so it's hard to keep your focus on the moment as you run. Gary's fast enough so he has to worry about things like that.

We made it through that section and started climbing the hills on Commonwealth Ave. Around mile 18, we were passed by a woman out on her own morning run. Gary and Ned couldn't have that, so they picked up their pace to keep up.

Brandon and I trailed along behind. After we reached the top of the last big hill, we started our own push in order to catch up.

It was still only 7 degrees according to a bank temperature sign when we caught up with Gary and Ned by Coolidge Corner. Our surges in the hills came back to haunt us soon thereafter. Brandon slowly dropped off the pace as we headed towards the finish, though he continued to make steady progress. Ned ran out of gas when we hit Kenmore Square, and he slowed to a walk in spite of the effect the cold and wind had on his sweaty body.

Just then we were hailed by Steve Vaitones, another member of SRR, who knew Gary from his role as a USATF-New England official. He had parked in Newton Center and was running back and forth on the course, looking for our group. He joined us, and Steve, Gary, and I trotted on. We turned onto Boylston St. and headed towards the finish when Gary decided it would be a good idea to head back to check on Brandon and Ned. I was ready to finish up and stop running, so I continued on with Steve as we ran over strings of beads left on the road from the previous night's celebration.

Steve and I crossed the finish line, about 4 hours after I left Hopkinton. We stood at the finish, waiting for the others to arrive. Brandon and Gary came in soon afterwards, but there was no Ned. Our sweaty clothes cooled almost instantly in the wind, so standing outside for long was an unpleasant proposition. Finally, shivering, we made our way back down the course, into the wind. We found Ned resting in the Boylston St. Starbucks, about a quarter-mile from the finish line.

Brandon's ride came to take him back to Hopkinton to get his car. The rest of us spread our damp gear around the coffee shop, refueled, and talked some more. One woman in the store had the Boston Globe. The top article in the Metro section was an interview of Gary conducted a few days before, about our upcoming run.

We stalled as long as we could before heading back out into the cold, but as tiredness caught up with us, the talk wound down. We put our cold, soggy clothes back on to leave. Gary and Ned headed to Gary's mother-in-law's place on nearby Clarendon St. Steve and I jogged into the wind, which felt even more bitter through our damp gear after the respite, to Copley Station. From there, Steve took the T to Newton for his car, and I headed back to Arlington.

So that's how I became the first person to finish the Boston Marathon course in 2009. I didn't actually get around to entering the actual race, but I take my victories wherever I can get them, and no one will ever be able to take this one away from me.

Running through the night on Deer Island in 2003

Chapter 8: Going Further - Ultras

"In my second ultra, a 50, the special moment was the decision to walk the last 8 miles. I had such ambivalent feelings about it. Was I a failure because I had to walk? A success because I was going to finish? After a few moments of considering those ideas, I got down to brass tacks and decided I was going to enjoy those last miles. I just decided to enjoy them. And I did."

- Adena Shutzberg

On a good day, I sometimes feel like I'd like to run forever. In 2003, I decided to see if I could.

By then, I had run a number of marathons and I was beginning to get a little frustrated. I'd train for a year to try and run a fast race, but when race day arrived the weather would be too hot or too windy or I would be injured, so running at a fast pace was impossible.

But I still wanted to improve as a runner. I still needed a goal, some focus for my training. I could continue to work on my speed, and make another attempt at a marathon or try to improve my time in shorter races. If I wanted to do that, I figured I'd need to work harder on speedwork. Speed training is hard on my body, though it does pay off. But whenever I spent much time focusing on speed, I seemed to get hurt.

I had another choice. I could try to run farther instead of faster. My running club, the Somerville Road Runners, puts on a 24-hour ultramarathon and relay every summer on a 5K loop course around Lake Quannapowitt in Wakefield, MA. I'd volunteered at the race and I was impressed by the persistence shown by the runners as they staggered past in the heat. I wondered about competing in the ultra myself someday, just to see how far I could go.

Ultramarathoning would be new and interesting. In some ways, running an ultra would be an easier choice than trying to beat my times at the shorter distances I'd been running. I didn't have to run faster. All I had to do was set a comfortable pace and keep going at that pace as long as I could. Every extra mile was a new PR.

Any run that's long enough to tire me out consists of three sections. In the first part of the run, I'm still fresh, but I might struggle some while I warm up and I'm trying to find a comfortable pace. Towards the end of the run, when I get tired, I need to fight through that to make it to the finish. Running to near exhaustion is necessary to build my endurance, and it's rewarding to meet the challenge, but it's not really lighthearted "fun".

Then there's the middle section of a run that starts when I've warmed up and I've settled into a relaxed groove. Running gets easy, fun, and the relentless drone/drumbeat of my feet quiets the babbling that usually goes on in my head. That part of the run is one of the best things about running, and the longer I run, the longer that middle section can be.

I decided it was worth the effort to try to run an ultramarathon. Now I needed a plan.

The Midsummer Lights Relay was scheduled for June 20th, which was the summer solstice and also my 42nd birthday. Tom Derderian and the Greater Boston Track Club invited teams of up to ten runners to race from dusk until dawn over a 3.05-mile course winding around Deer Island in Boston Harbor. The team completing the most laps wins.

For the first time, people from SRR were putting together some teams to participate in the event. I was sitting at my computer, reading the messages on the club email list as the teams were organizing, and on the spur of the moment (more or less), I decided to run the race by myself.

The race seemed like a good way to ease into ultrarunning (if such a thing is possible). I thought it was a good idea to try a loop course first, so I didn't have to worry about whether I'd have easy access to food, drinks, dry socks, or anything else I needed throughout the race. And if anything went wrong, I wouldn't be any farther than a mile-and-a-half away from help.

I got in touch with Tom the Monday before the race. Since my relay team would consist of only one person, Tom kindly agreed to allow me in with a reduced entry fee, and so Team Ibuprofen was born.

I didn't give the race a lot of advance thought before signing up, so my training for it consisted of the base I developed while training for marathons. I had run five in the two years before the ultra, and a good number of 20-28 mile runs while I was preparing for them. The Boston Marathon in April 2003 was my most recent one. My only long run after that was a slow, meandering 30-mile run along Boston Harbor two weeks before the ultra, which I ran mostly so I could play with my new Timex GPS. That 30 miles was the farthest I'd ever run.

After I registered for the race, I spent the rest of the week having a wonderful time planning what I'd need to bring with me. I researched how to run ultras on the Internet and made lists of supplies that might come in handy.

I ended up packing a ton of stuff, way more than I'd need, organized into bags for easy access. I had a bag of food, a bag of medical supplies, a bag of extra clothing, a bag of "other stuff" (an MP3 player and other distractions), a couple extra pairs of shoes, and a cooler full of drinks and ice. I even packed a tent, in case I got tired and needed to rest.

Thursday, I went out for my traditional pre-race short haircut so I'd be as cool as possible and to help me focus on the task ahead of me. Then Friday finally arrived. I left work at about 1 PM, had a big lunch, and went home to pack and take a short nap. I dressed the same way I would for a normal long run. I put Bodyglide on my thighs as usual. I also stuck a Compeed on the hotspot on the ball of my right foot to avoid blistering. The finishing touch was the headlamp my wife gave me for my birthday just before I headed out.

At about 6:45, I got in the car and drove to Deer Island. The island, formerly the site of a jail, now hosts a modern sewage treatment plant and a small park. I parked my car at the bottom of a hill, and then I walked up a path to meet Tom at the registration table on top of the hill. He showed me an article he'd written about my ultra attempt for the Winthrop paper. That was a bit odd – no one had ever used me to advertise a race before.

Runners who were part of a team had a lot of downtime during the night to look forward to while they waited for their turn to run, so they pitched tents around the park and settled in. I decided to go without a tent because the weather was pleasant, just about ideal for a June race. It was clear (unusual that spring), in the 60's, and there was hardly any wind.

Like most small races, things were pretty informal. There were no bib numbers or timing clocks. Tom gave each of the 10 teams a multi-colored light wand to use as a relay baton. The wands were fun toys, but they turned off automatically every 10 minutes. All night long, we had to keep turning the wands back on while we ran.

At about 8:25, as the sun set, Tom played "Taps" on a harmonica. We all stood there waiting until he said, "That's it – you can get started now," and then we took off.

I went out at a comfortable pace, running the first lap alongside some of the slower relay runners while I learned the course. I planned on slowing down as the night went on.

The start/finish line was at registration, on the peak of the highest hill on the island. From there, the course wound gradually downhill, past the parking area at the bottom, around the island, and back up to the start. The course was mostly concrete sidewalk, with some asphalt sections in the park. There was some dirt alongside the concrete, but I decided not to risk twisting an ankle. There was one other small hill early in the loop around the island. There was a sharp turn at the bottom of that hill that got more difficult as the night went on.

At the end of the first mile, the SRR relay teams set up camp on a flat, grassy space near the entrance to the sewage plant. Mile two went through the sewage plant on some fenced-in paths, and then around the southern tip of the island. Mile three ran alongside a breakwater on the eastern shore before turning to go up the hill back to the start.

There was quite a contrast in the views, depending on which way I turned my head. As I ran counter-clockwise around the island, to my right was Boston Harbor, with beautiful views of the Boston skyline, ships, the ocean, and Winthrop. To the left, the Deer Island Waste Water Treatment Plant was interesting in its own, industrial-technical-institutional way, with 170-foot-high egg-shaped digesters adding an other-worldly touch. Luckily, the sewage plant didn't add any special odor to the event.

After the first lap, I began to use a tip I had read online. I alternated 5 minutes of running with 1 minute of walking to make it easier for me to keep going for an extended period. I also walked the 89 yards from the 3-mile marker up to the finish line, the steepest part of the course.

My main goal, the one I told to my friends, was to still be running at dawn. I had dreams of completing 50 miles (actually 52, since only complete laps counted towards my score). That would require averaging 30 minutes per lap. If I did it, great, but I wasn't going to risk doing a crash-and-burn to meet that goal in my first ultra.

Once I began walking, I lost contact with the rest of the runners. It got dark, and a booze-cruise appeared offshore. The lights on the ship added to the festivities, but the loud karaoke was annoying. The party shut down around midnight. After that, we ran on in relative quiet.

I mostly ran on my own through the night. Ten runners (fewer after some teams dropped out) scattered over more than three miles didn't make for much company. Every time I passed the SRR encampment, I got cheers and offers of beer, and those perked me up. I also looked forward to the attaboys I got each time I climbed the hill to the scoring table, and to coasting downhill for a bit after that. SRR's Eric Forgy did his weekend long run on the course (he ended up doing 7 laps) and he ran with me for a while.

The rest of the time I was alone except for relay runners going by and some people who were fishing along the eastern shore. I was surprised by how long the fishermen stayed out there, well into the early morning. Still, I expect they were much more surprised by the runners continually passing through their normally quiet fishing spot.

Most of the course was lit well enough. There was a dark patch at the southern end, with an eerie beep emanating from the shadows to warn off boats. There was another dark section along the eastern breakwater, just before the turn to climb up to the finish. I could see the reflection of my headlamp in the eyes of the animals clambering around out there. I never figured out what animals they were.

I stopped at the car every two laps to top off my water bottle. I visited the Port-a Bush regularly throughout the night, which showed I was drinking enough. I was drinking Accelerade, which has a 4/1 carbohydrate/protein mix. The protein in the mix was supposed to help keep my body from burning muscles for fuel.

After 18 miles, I started taking GU each time I refilled my bottle. I munched on a few almonds at most of the later pit stops, mostly for salt, but partly because I'd read the Vitamin E in almonds was good during a long race. Other than that, I didn't have much to eat. The bagels, Power Bars, and beef jerky stayed in the bag. I wasn't nauseous, but the idea of food wasn't very appealing.

Towards the end of the night, the Accelerade began to bother my stomach. I kept refilling my bottle with Accelerade, but I started drinking water with my snacks at the stops and that helped some.

I had a couple of ibuprofen before the start. I had two more at about three and six hours into the race. I also had a few electrolyte pills as the night wore on, and I refreshed the Bodyglide on my thighs as needed.

The running went pretty well. I kept under 30 minutes per lap for the first 20 miles or so, but I knew that wouldn't last the whole way. The 7th and 8th laps were a transition period. After that, I slowed down to a 10 minute/mile pace when I was running. Even with running slower, the walking, and the breaks at the car, each lap still took less than 35 minutes. I felt I'd be able to keep to that pace as long as I could keep running at all.

The pain from the pounding built up to a certain point, but never got too bad as long as I kept my form. If I started to sit back on my heels too much, the ITB in my right knee would remind me to stop. My achilles tendons were a little more sore than usual, but it wasn't unmanageable.

Staying alert was less of a problem than I had feared. What got to be a problem as the night wore on was staying motivated. I ran into a small, cold patch of fog every so often and that would pick me up a little bit, but the feeling faded quickly. The rest of the time I knew I could keep running, but I sometimes had trouble remembering why I wanted to. I started to let myself walk up the shorter hill, and my regular walking breaks began to stretch on for 15-20 seconds past the beeping of my watch before I went back to running.

When I reached the end of another lap at 2:30 in the morning, Tom asked me if I needed anything. I muttered "Dawn," and then I headed wearily down the hill yet again.

I made it through 13 laps (about 40 miles), and then it was late enough in the race to begin planning for the end. I knew I could get in two more laps, but adding a third lap would be tough. If that last lap would have gotten me over 50 miles, I might have gone for it. Given the situation, I decided to leave well enough alone and just make sure I finished two more.

Along the backstretch of the second-to-last lap, the sky finally lightened in the east. Bob Ross from SRR pulled up alongside during a walking break. He stayed to chat with me and that helped get me through the next running section and to the end of the lap.

On the last lap, I picked up my pace a bit since I knew I was finally almost done, but I was very careful to make sure I ran slowly enough so that running one more lap was out of the question. As I passed the SRR camp, I asked Joe O'Leary to meet me at the finish to take a picture, since I was sure he would get there faster than I could.

Finally, after 8 hours, 7 minutes, and 10 seconds and 46 (well, 45.758) miles, I was through! I stopped on the hilltop at the finish and stood there, basking in the feeling of not running. That feeling was interrupted almost immediately by an attacking swarm of mosquitoes, but once again Bob Ross came through. He lent me his long-sleeved shirt for protection and we took the trip down to the SRR camp. Everyone was packing up to leave, but I wasn't quite ready to go so I went by myself back up to the finish to watch the dawn.

The race ended when the sun came up. It was a fine, sunny spring morning. I had no idea who won, where they were from, or how many laps they finished, nor did I care. I just stood there, enjoying the view from the hill as the morning sun reflected off the ocean and the Boston skyline, and enjoying my well-earned sense of accomplishment.

I survived the race without any blisters and with only minor chafing on my thighs. The next day I was a little sorer than I would usually be after a marathon, but I ran slow enough that I didn't feel all beat up. I rested for a few days, and then Tuesday morning I went out for an easy 3-mile run. In comparison, it seemed to go by in no time at all!

By the next week, I felt fully recovered and ready to go back to my normal routine while I figured out what I wanted to do next. I still hadn't found how far I could go, and after my success on Deer Island, I was ready to push things further.

A 50-mile race seemed like a good next step. I found the Vermont 50 online. It's a trail race for runners and mountain bikers that's held in September. There's also a 50K on a shortened version of the course.

I grew up in Vermont and I always liked going back there to run. Traveling to the race wouldn't be hard. Running on softer dirt trails seemed like it might be easier on my body. So I signed up and started training.

Race day was about two-and-a-half months away. I didn't really do anything special before the Midsummer Night Relay, so I didn't plan much extra training for Vermont. I decided to use the SRR 24 Hour Ultra on August 1st as a training run, and that would be my only really long effort before September.

I wanted to finish recovering from Midsummer Nights and go into the 24 Hour rested, so I didn't do any long runs in July. I did enter a few shorter races. Towards the end of July, I did two 10Ks in one day, something I had never done before. I was in Vermont on vacation and I ran a 10K in Swanton in the morning. After the race, I was talking to some Canadians who were heading down to Goshen for the trail race at the Blueberry Hill ski area. I knew from doing that race twice before that it was a monstrously hilly course, but I felt good and thought it would be good training for the 50, so I went, had a lot of fun, and beat my previous best time for the race by two minutes. I noticed that I recovered quickly from those races, something I credited to extra endurance from ultrarunning.

I also started doing some running on the trails in the Middlesex Fells near my home. Those trails aren't mountainous, but they do have plenty of the difficult footing I needed to prepare for the 50. I learned from running on the rocks and roots in the Fells that I needed shoes that were more protective than my regular running shoes. I bought a pair of trail shoes with a hard plastic plate in the sole and a built-in gaiter to keep trail debris out. They weren't terribly comfortable and the gaiter made it hard to get the shoes on and off, but they worked well on the trail.

For the 24 Hour, I was the first runner for a relay team made up of people from SRR doing their long training runs, one after the other. I started when the gun went off at 7PM and ran through the night. I completed 14 laps around the lake for a total of 44.2 miles before I handed off the baton. Even though everybody on the team was running at a leisurely long run pace, we finished as the first place mixed team. It did help that we were the *only* mixed team.

I fit in two more 22-mile long runs before it was time to go to Vermont. By now I'd built up enough endurance so that 22 miles was far enough to be a good workout, but not far enough to wipe me out. I ran the last one three weeks before the race. The day after I finished that run, I felt good enough to take the risk of jumping into a 3-mile race. I had never dared to race so soon after a long run before. I surprised myself and ran a 19:15, which would have been a pretty good time for me even if it wasn't right after a 22-mile run.

My training was going well, but I managed to find plenty of other concerns to keep myself busy. Like always, I wanted to have as much as possible planned in advance. Then when race day arrived, I could just follow my checklist and I wouldn't have to worry about forgetting anything.

The race was going to start and finish at the Ascutney Mountain lodge, so I got a room there for the night before and the night after the race. The room wasn't cheap, but if I stayed there, I could be sure I would make it to the start on time, and I knew I'd have a place to collapse afterwards if I needed it.

I asked Mark Bates and Karen Matteson, friends of mine who lived in Vermont, if they wanted to help out by meeting me at various places on the course to restock my supplies. I wanted my own sports drink, the Accelerade with the extra protein, and I wanted the energy gels I was used to, but I didn't want to carry along a whole day's supply. I also wanted the comfort of knowing there would be friendly faces along the way to cheer me on. Mark and Karen signed on as my crew, and we spent some time printing maps and directions and going over them to plan how we would get together before and during the race.

I took a look at the list of "stuff to bring to an ultra" that I made before Midsummer Nights. Now that I had a little experience, I was able to cut out some items I knew I wouldn't need. Then I added even more things back in. I was going to be running on trails a long way from anywhere, so I wanted to make sure I'd have everything I could possibly need.

The race allowed me to have a pacer run with me for the last 8 miles if I wanted. I thought about asking someone to pace for me in case I needed the help, but I finally decided that was one thing I could do without.

I drove up to Brownsville, VT the day before the race. I wasn't worried, but I was anxious. I wanted to know whether all my training and planning was going to pay off.

When I got to the Ascutney Mountain lodge, I stood outside for a minute, surrounded by forest-covered mountains, and I soaked in the autumnal beauty. When I lived in Vermont, I took the fall foliage for granted, sometimes even resenting it as a harbinger of winter. Now, it was glorious to see.

Then it struck me. "Yikes! I'm about to run 50 miles, and there's nothing around here but mountains."

I checked in to the lodge, and then I went down to pick up my race number and t-shirt. This race was important to me, so I wanted a memento. I splurged on a fleece shirt with the VT 50 logo. I took it all back to the room, and then I tried to get some rest before dinner.

The race committee puts on a meal for the runners and the bikers at the Brownsville town hall the night before the race. The only other option in town to help pass the time was a visit to the general store, so I went to the dinner. For the most part, I sat and listened while I ate. I was amused by how easy it was to tell the bikers from the runners, partly because the bikers were more gregarious, but mostly because the bikers looked fit, with muscular legs, while the ultrarunners looked like they could use an extra serving or two of food. The major topic for both groups was the forecast for race day, which called for lots of rain.

I woke up before dawn Sunday morning and I went to the start for the 5:30 AM pre-race meeting and a pre-race snack. I was wired up, excited to finally be at the start, and ready to go. The anxiety was a good feeling, unlike the pre-race jitters I had to deal with while I was worrying about whether I was doing everything I needed to do to prepare. No more decisions, no time for doubts. All I had left to do was run.

At 6:15, the first wave of bikers took off. The remaining bikes left, and then the runners followed at 6:40AM. It was about 60 degrees and cloudy, good running weather - if the rain held off.

My only goal was to finish, so I started at the back of the pack. I began by alternating 5 minutes of running at a comfortable pace with 1 minute of walking, a plan that had served me fairly well at Midsummer Nights and the 24 Hour. But those races were in the Boston area, on relatively flat urban courses. When I got to the first long uphill section, I started running up. Then I took another look at the mountains and I realized that there was no way that I could run up all of them at anything resembling "a comfortable pace". I changed my strategy to another I'd read about online. Instead of running by my watch, I started running the downhills and the few flat stretches and I conserved my energy by walking up the mountain trails.

I was about five miles into the race, about an hour after the start, when it began to rain. By the time I reached the third aid station, about 12 miles into the race, the rain had turned into a downpour. It was the first of the three aid stations where crews were allowed to meet their runners, so Mark and Karen were waiting there, trying to stay dry in their car. When they saw me, they jumped out into the rain, refilled my bottle, and asked me if I wanted dry socks. I thought about it, but in the heavy rain changing socks seemed pointless.

It got worse. The rain wasn't the biggest problem, though I was soaked through for the rest of the day. The biggest problem was mud. When you take hours of pouring rain and dirt trails in the mountains and add mountain bikes to churn up the trails, you get mud, lots of it. Within a short time, everyone but the lead bikers was wallowing in a sea of mud.

For a while, I tried to avoid the worst of the mud and water as I ran along. But that was impossible. Finally, I came up to yet another lake of mud of indeterminate depth. I looked down at it, and I gave up. Instead of making even a token effort to keep my feet clean and dry, I just plowed straight through. It was oddly liberating.

Later on, there wasn't any option. To get ahead, I had to wade (or slide, if I was going downhill) through the mud, which had been churned by the bikes to the point where it was often shin-deep. From time to time, I'd smash my toes into rocks buried out of sight underneath the surface of the mud. I was thankful for my trail shoes. Some people had their shoes sucked off their feet, but the gaiters built into my shoes had a death grip on my feet, so my shoes stayed on while I plowed through the mud.

At one point, on an unusually steep uphill section, the mud was so slippery that I couldn't get enough traction to make the climb. I had to stop and find a stick long enough and sturdy enough so I could jam it in the mud deep enough and use it as a support as I climbed.

It was tough on the runners, but even worse for the bikers who weren't at the front of the pack. Their bikes couldn't make it up the hills in the mud, and it wasn't safe for them to plow downhill, since they were totally out of control. A lot of riders quit. I passed some of the ones who didn't, doggedly carrying their bikes over their shoulders as they trudged towards the finish.

Coming into aid stations was always fun. They were the only markers to show me where I was on the course. My favorite aid stations were located on mountaintop meadows, where they provided a short respite after a long climb. At the aid stations, I could have a shot of energy gel, refill my bottle, and get a bit of encouragement from the volunteers before heading on.

I kept it simple, and stuck with gels and sports drink throughout the race. They were enough to keep me going so I didn't have any real bad patches where I ran out of gas. Other people ate the solid food available at the stations. Things were going well enough that I didn't want to risk an upset stomach, though the smell of the hot soup at one station was very tempting!

I was pleased with how well I held to my pace. In an ultramarathon, most people settle into their own pace and just keep going, never speeding up much. Unless you're up front, the race is more about competing with yourself to hold on as long as you can instead of trying to outdo the other runners. If you can keep going, inevitably you'll start to pass people.

Starting at about 20 miles, I began to pass some of the people I'd let go at the beginning of the race. Whenever I saw someone appear ahead of me, there was no urgency to catch them. I knew that if I stayed patient and kept doing what I was doing it was just a matter of time before I'd run them down. That was very satisfying. In the meantime, they were helping pull me along. I wasn't going to win anything, but I felt like I was managing my race well.

The course was well marked most of the way around. There were yellow tags with black arrows to direct me around turns, and to reassure me that I was on the correct path.

At one point in the middle of the race, a downhill stretch of single-track trail fed into a dirt road at an angle. The correct route was a sharp cut back to the right, one that was impossible for a bike to take at full speed. As I approached the turn, a bike whizzed by and zoomed off in the wrong direction, followed by two runners. When I got to the turn and figured out that they'd headed off incorrectly, I was able to yell loudly enough to get them to turn around.

The positive karma I built up there didn't keep me from getting lost later in the race. I was cruising along a road, pulling ahead of a couple of runners I'd caught up with at the sixth aid station. I hadn't seen a yellow tag for some time, but I wasn't worried until I saw a police car in the road ahead of me with its flashers going. That was usually a sign of a crossing, not just a turn. At the same time, I could just hear the runners behind me yelling. I turned and saw them waving, back up at the top of the hill I'd just descended.

I realized that I must have missed a turn somewhere, and headed back uphill. Unfortunately, by the time I got back, the runners who had been following me had disappeared. I continued on, hoping to find the correct turn, but I never did.

As I backtracked, the road became less familiar, making me think I might not be retracing my path correctly. I was relieved to see a biker off in the woods to my left. I asked him where he was on the course, and he told me he was about a half-mile past the seventh aid station. According to the rules, I was supposed to get back on the trail where I got off. I decided I would get on the trail where the biker was and head backwards until I made it to where I lost the trail, and then I'd turn around. By doing that, at least I'd know I was on the trail somewhere, not wandering lost in the mountains.

I ran up and down a few hills and backwards through the seventh aid station, running in the opposite direction of a number of very surprised runners and bikers. After a few miles, I started to get anxious about finding the right spot to turn. By now, I'd run over 30 miles forwards and a couple miles backwards, and I was not thinking as clearly as I needed to. I got to the road crossing with the police car where I first realized I'd gotten lost, which meant I'd done a big loop and I still didn't know how far I had to go to get back to where I first got lost. Since I didn't really know where I'd left the trail, I talked myself into thinking I'd spent enough time wandering around, and I turned and started towards the finish.

A few people passed me soon after I started heading forward again. That made me think that I might have skipped ahead and gotten in with some faster runners. I figured I'd worry about finishing first, and sort out the results later.

I was now 35 miles into the race, and I was starting to slow down some. The aid stations began to seem farther apart than I expected. Trying to run on the hard surfaces was painful. When I reached a section of the course that was on asphalt or hard-packed dirt roads, I could feel every step, from my hips all the way down through the soles of my feet. Early in the race, it had been nice to get out of the mud and run freely for a while. But running in pliant mud has its benefits. By the end of the race, pain was making me run just as slowly on the roads as I ran in the mud. What was a pretty good pace in the mud was just a slow plod out on the road.

People always ask about the pain. "Doesn't it hurt?" ranks above even "You're crazy," and only slightly behind "I could never do that" in the list of things people say when I talk with non-runners about ultrarunning. Yes, it hurts, but it's almost always pain I can ignore and keep going. Pain that I ignore long enough goes away, usually when it's replaced by other pains.

I spent the final ten miles of the race slogging along, passing and being passed by Audrey Rue Nelson from Oregon. We waded through more mud, climbed more mountains, forded flash floods in the valleys between the mountains, and made silly remarks as we passed each other. I ended up finishing about 20 seconds ahead of her. I know it helped me to have someone to run with for the last stretch of the race. I hope it helped her just as much, because later I found that she really should have finished ahead of me.

Just when I was wondering if the race would ever end, I came out of a patch of woods and found myself running across a field on the side of a mountain with the finish line finally in sight down below. I took one last slip and fall on the wet grass, then ran down the hill and crossed the finish line, after ten hours, one minute, and 22 seconds.

I stopped in the finish chute and just stood there stunned, wet, and coated in mud up to my knees. I had to readjust to having to think about what I needed to do next, rather than mindlessly engaging in RFP (Relentless Forward Progress). Mark and Karen were there to help me get my jacket on and start moving again. I poked at the post-race barbeque without really feeling hungry, and then we went back to the hotel, out of the rain at last. Mark and Karen went home, while I went in for a shower, a bit of food, and a beer.

I got in the shower, hosed off the mud, and took stock. In spite of all the water and mud in my shoes, I only had one blister, which hadn't bothered me at all during the race. My feet were more beaten than usual, after bouncing off more than one rock buried in the mud. They were somewhat swollen and bruised, with some scrapes on the inside of both ankles from the opposite shoe rubbing against them while I ran. The left foot was a bit more battered, with two black toenails and some skin worn off between the toes. All in all, I came through the race pretty well. My legs were a bit more tired than they would be after a marathon, but recovery followed my normal pattern and by Thursday I could walk down stairs without holding on to the railing.

The mud was memorable. The next year, at the 2004 race, they were selling muddy brown "I survived the 2003 Vermont 50" t-shirts. After he finished the race, Sean Smith posted online that "I'd never seen mud do some of the things I saw it do yesterday." Doug Freese, who had run in all of the previous Vermont 50s, wrote, "Never here, or at any other place for that matter, had I experienced these conditions for such an extended time." Doug figures he lost about an hour-and-a-half to the mud.

The week after the race was over I got the splits from the timing company. They showed that while I was getting back on the trail after I got lost, I went from 29th place at the sixth station to 20th at the seventh station. I compared my time for the seventh leg to other runners who were going at a similar pace, and I figured that I'd probably cut my total time down by about 25 minutes by skipping parts of the course, even with all the backtracking.

Because I hadn't run the correct course, I emailed the race director and disqualified myself. That hurt a bit, but even if no one else knew, I would have known that I'd cut things short, and I couldn't let myself get away with that. The race director fixed the results in one update, then lost track somehow while making another update. I'm not that much of a saint, and it's not like I won anything, so I left it at that and today I show up as a finisher in the results posted online.

In spite of my problems, I was very happy with my race. Running on the mountain trails was much harder than the runs at Midsummer Nights and the 24 Hour, but the course was beautiful when I found time to look around, even in the rain. I had an immense amount of fun dealing with all the challenges of the race, and I had a really good stretch of calm, meditative running going before I got lost. And I was still running when I crossed the finish line, so I still hadn't found out how far I could go.

At the finish of the 2003 Vermont 50 – finally!

Chapter 9: Going Even Further

"There's a tremendous synergy for me between running and meditation. To be a better runner, you need to listen to your body, stay focused, be aware when emotions are pulling you away from your race or training plan, prioritize long-term goals over short-term distractions, all things that meditation specifically trains you to become better at.

At the same time, at least for me, running has helped with the meditation. It's a lot of hours per week when I'm practicing meditation rather than being busy with all the distractions of work and home life. It provides direct feedback that I'm disconnected or caught up in worries or planning, and a really simple way back towards being present. It relaxes the body and generates great energy, both of which are really important for engaging with the mind."

- John Chapin

After the rush of finishing the Vermont 50, I was a little adrift. Ultrarunning opened up a whole new set of options, so I had more to think about while I figured out what my next goal would be.

I wasn't really interested in the sort of work it would take to get faster in shorter races, like 5Ks and 10Ks. I had plenty of room for improvement there, but I was enjoying running long much more than I ever liked track workouts or speed intervals on the road.

I could go back to the marathon and try using my new-found endurance there to go faster. That was very tempting. I only had to beat my marathon PR by three minutes to reach 3:10, the open qualifying time for Boston. That was something I'd wanted to do for years. Who knew what else was possible?

I could run 50 miles. Maybe a three hour marathon was within my reach?

Still, racing marathons was essentially the same thing I had been doing for years before I tried ultrarunning. New achievements were harder to come by, and I wasn't getting the same kick out of them as I did when I was starting out.

I found running 50 miles to be more rewarding. I got internal satisfaction from reaching a difficult goal. I also got the sort of external recognition from my running friends that I never had before. I wasn't slow, but I would never be fast enough in marathons or shorter races to impress our group. In ultramarathoning, I had found a way to do something that intrigued most of the other runners I knew, and I liked that.

Still, the praise I received made me a little uncomfortable. I loved getting it, and it helped me enjoy what I'd accomplished, but it also made me want to go even further to show that I really deserved it.

In a strange way, it was easier to run 50 miles than it was to run 26.2. Since my only goal was to complete the distance, I didn't have to worry that I wasn't as physically gifted as some of the other runners. There was no time pressure, and all I needed was persistence. That made it feel like I had more control over my ultrarunning success. Barring injury, it was up to me whether I'd keep going, and so far, I was always able to do that.

I could try for a faster 50-mile race, but that just got me back in the same rut of worrying about speed. Alternatively, I could continue to push the distance to see how far I could run. The 50-mile race was tough, but I could have run farther. I knew that there must be a limit somewhere, and I was curious what it would be.

If I was going to run farther, I wanted to do it on trails. In spite of the rain and mud, Vermont taught me that I enjoyed running long distances on the trails much more than I liked running similar distances on asphalt or concrete.

I went back online to search for my next race. I didn't find many trail ultramarathons longer than 50 miles to choose from. Most of the choices were located outside of easy driving range, but there was a 100-mile race in Vermont in July. One hundred miles would be a big step up, but that race was by far the most convenient option.

I wasn't sure what my training plan should be. The only change I had made to my marathon training schedule before entering the 50-mile race was to add in an extra-long run once every month or so. I never ran the entire race distance in training, but it turned out that I didn't need to. On race day, instead of trying to go faster, I merely tried to go farther, and it worked.

I didn't see how my training runs could get much longer. My 40-45 mile runs took eight or nine hours to complete. Longer runs would take an awful lot of time, and might require enough recovery time afterwards that I'd end up running fewer miles overall. I knew if I kept to my current schedule, I was capable of running more than 50 miles. Hopefully, another eight or nine months of that would be enough to get me ready for a try at the Vermont 100. I was just going to have to extend my range even farther on race day in order to reach 100 miles.

My "plan" left me plenty of time to enter some short races along the way to have some fun and spend some time hanging out with my friends. Those races could also serve as speedwork for a marathon. I figured why not try to do both Boston and the Vermont 100? I knew I would definitely have plenty of endurance, and I was qualified for Boston from my finish at Cape Cod in 2002. The marathon was in April, which left plenty of time for me to recover before trying Vermont in July.

I started training again about a month after the Vermont 50, in November 2003. I was in Virginia on a business trip, and I extended the trip into the weekend so I could run the Potomac Heritage Trail 50K. I knew I wanted to add more trail running to my training, and my long runs were much more fun when I could do them in a race with other people.

The 50K started and finished at a home in the Georgetown section of Washington, DC. We had to run a few miles on roads to escape the urban starting area. After that most of the course was dirt, on the Heritage Trail system and the canal path alongside the Potomac River.

It was an informal race, with trail marking to match. The group I was running with at the start of the race got lost while we were still in Georgetown. Once we found our way back on course, the pack started to split up. I decided I would drop back to run the rest of the race with the people going at a slower pace to ensure I could keep up. It was just a training run for me, and I wanted to make sure I was running with someone who knew where they were going, or at least make sure I wouldn't be alone if we got lost again.

That paid off at the end of the race when the group I was with got lost because of poor course markings again. This time, while we were trying to get back on track, we came across the reason for the problem. A boy was carrying a handful of ribbons that he had pulled down from the section of the course the ribbons were supposed to be marking. Luckily, my local guides were still able to lead me to the finish.

Between the leisurely pace and getting lost twice, it took me a little over 7 hours to finish the race. I had fun, and because of the slow pace I was able to continue training without a break, even after running over 30 miles.

The calendar turned to 2004. I did one 42-mile run on the roads at the end of January. The rest of the time I averaged about 40 miles per week, with 18-22 mile runs on the weekends.

That took me to mid-February and the Martha's Vineyard 20 miler, part of a traditional New England race series that leads up to Boston in April. I ran Martha's Vineyard without going all out and I still managed to run it at a 7:05 pace. It was a flat course, but I was running into the teeth of a 20-30 mph wind for half of the race, so when I was done, I felt good about my progress towards the marathon.

After the Vineyard race, I fit in one 27-mile run and a couple of other 20-mile runs. I mixed in a few rest weeks and a couple of short races. My times in the races were good enough to make me start dreaming that I might have a chance at breaking 3:10 in Boston.

The weather leading up to the marathon had been typical for spring in New England. April temperatures hovered in the 40s. But the day before the marathon, the thermometer jumped into the 60s. Race day was worse. It was hot, sunny, and humid. The temperature in Boston rose to 86, a record high for the date.

At the start, I knew that I wasn't going to be able to run the fast time I'd hoped for, but I still thought I might be able to overcome the heat and run a time that would qualify me for next year's race. That idea lasted for about 8 miles before the heat forced me to slow down. By the Newton hills, I was slogging along at more than 10 minutes per mile. I had gotten a bag of ice from a spectator and tied it to my head to try and keep me cool. I finished in 3:46:12, but at least I finished, and I didn't end my race with an IV in my arm the way hundreds of other runners did.

Boston was a major disappointment, but the race had still served a useful purpose by distracting me from the Vermont

100. I took two weeks to recover from the marathon, and then I put it behind me and got back to training for the ultra.

Four weeks after Boston, I went on another Virginia business trip and made a side trip to West Virginia for the Capon Valley 50k. Capon Valley was a very tough course on steep mountain trails. I was happy to reach the finish still running well after averaging a 10-minute pace, so I rewarded myself with a pleasant dip in the Capon River afterwards to cool off.

I went on another business trip at the end of May, this time to San Diego. The Rock and Roll Marathon was scheduled for the following week, which was six weeks before Vermont. I extended my stay by using some vacation time, and I used the race for one last long run.

I found plenty of people in the area to run with while I was out west. The weekend before the marathon I went with a group from the Movin' Shoes store to the mountains north of the city where we ran 12 miles at an elevation of about 4,500 feet on the trails in the Cuyamaca Rancho State Park. San Diego has a very active Hash House Harrier community, so during the week I was able to run trail with three different hashes. I also did a little running by myself along the ocean, but mostly I enjoyed running in new places guided by friendly new people.

On marathon day I got up early and ran 11 miles before the race started. Then I jogged a mile up to the starting area and ran the marathon, for a total of 38 miles on the day.

It was the first marathon I'd run without worrying about my time. That let me relax and enjoy the experience. I even felt free to stop running and lose 10 minutes early in the race, when I went into a bagel shop for a bathroom break.

A mob of almost 20,000 people carried me along the course. Many of them were dressed in Team in Training purple and running their first marathon for the Leukemia Society. The last six miles of the race were tough after the pounding from running more than 30 miles on asphalt, so instead of jogging two more miles, I declared it a day when I reached the finish line and I took the shuttle bus back to my hotel. My time of 3:49 would have been about average for a typical Boston, but here among the charity runners it put me in the top 10 percent.

It would be hard to find an event more different from the trail ultramarathons I'd been doing than the Rock and Roll Marathon. The trail races were low-key events. The advertised course lengths were "close enough," but no one was surprised if the trail was a mile or two shorter or longer than advertised. Experienced runners show up ready to go out and run alone on a tough course for long stretches. They accept the chance that they might get lost and add an extra mile to the race while trying to get back on track. There's camaraderie among the runners and all the necessary support from the race organizers, but most of the runners are inwardly focused and prepared to take care of themselves.

On the other hand, the marathon was an enormous spectacle targeted towards the needs and desires of the first-timers and charity runners. There were bands and teams of cheerleaders posted every mile to provide entertainment, coaches and pace group leaders traveling the course to push runners along, frequent water stops with plenty of port-a-potties, Marines manning the finish with medals, towels soaked in refreshing ice water, food, medical care for those who needed it, shuttles to take you wherever you need to go in the city, and a big concert after the race featuring the band Live. An assortment of souvenirs was available, including photos and even video of each runner as they crossed the finish line.

Still, at the core there are similarities between the two races. Most of the entrants in both events are there in spite of the fact that they have no chance of winning. They expect to discover things about themselves by pushing to their limits. They just have very different sets of limits to push.

After the San Diego trip, I went home to finish my training and to indulge in the feverish planning that was by now part of my regular pre-race routine. Mark Bates and Karen Matteson were going to be my crew again, like they were for the 50. That was a big help to me while I was preparing my gear. I could have them carry whatever I thought I might need, rather than limiting myself to what I could pack into a few small drop bags.

Three weeks before Vermont, I set a new 10K PR at Whirlaway. That was nice, but a 10K PR was so totally irrelevant to the goal I was working on that I barely noticed it.

Two weeks before Vermont, I did one last 22-mile run. After that, I rested, running no more than six miles (usually only four) every other day. This left plenty of time for obsessive planning, and I took full advantage. The upcoming race was the only thing on my mind. I had no idea whether I had trained enough to be ready to run 100 miles, but I was going to find out.

In every race, I have a goal that I share with people and a tougher goal that I keep to myself. That's how I try to manage expectations, especially my own. My main goal for this race was to finish. That would be challenge enough. There's a 30-hour cutoff, so if I didn't finish by then (or if I was behind the 30-hour pace when I reached an aid station) my race was over. Anyone who finishes under 24 hours wins a belt buckle. I knew that if I could keep running the whole way, I'd have a reasonably good chance of "buckling," but I still wasn't sure just how far I actually could run.

The Tuesday before the race, I went for my race haircut. I had it cut shorter than it'd been since my father was the one telling the barber what to do. It's something I've done for other races, but never to that extent. I knew it was silly while I was doing it, but I still did it, and I felt a little better because of it.

Mid-July arrived and it was time to leave for Vermont. Step one of the plan was to leave from work mid-day Thursday for the trip to Woodstock. That would give me all day Friday to rest and try to relax before the start of the race early Saturday morning.

The relaxing part wasn't going well. I was wound up, worrying about whether I was as ready as I could be, and searching for any last-minute task that might help in some slight way. I wasn't totally satisfied with the running shoes I had on hand, so I decided to stop at the New Balance outlet on the way north and see if I could find a better pair of trail shoes. I knew it would be stupid to try a brand new shoe out for the first time during the race, but I ended up buying a pair of model 870 trail shoes, even though they didn't really fit that well, just so I could Do Something. Then, a little further along on the trip, I stopped the car to go on a little test run with the new shoes. I jogged back and forth, dithering about whether I should wear the shoes during the race, until I got it together enough to realize that what I needed to do most was get back in the car and finish the trip.

I got to the motel, unloaded the car, and took a look around. The motel had twelve rooms, about half of which were taken by other runners. I met the owner of the motel and her daughter. They were talking with a couple who had first stayed there 12 years ago, when the owner had just learned she was pregnant with her daughter. The couple had come back to the motel for the race every year since then, part of a group of runners who have stayed there for the race year after year.

Friday morning after breakfast I went to the start at Silver Hill Meadow to register. The organizers had mowed a wide area in the meadow for the race and the competitors to use. In the middle of the space there were a few large tents for the official race activities. To either side, runners who were camping out at the start set up a number of smaller tents and campers. There were also small grazing areas staked out for each horse that would be participating in the race, with the horses' trailers and a tent or camper for the riders and their friends next to them.

I went in the main tent and picked up my number and t-shirt. Then I turned in the donations I'd collected for the race charity, Vermont Adaptive Ski & Sports. I usually don't try to compete with other runners for donations. I know a lot of runners, and we all get lots of requests to support charity efforts, so many that we can't respond to all of them. This time I figured that a 100-mile race was a special occasion that would stand out from the rest of the crowd, and it was for a cause that didn't have hordes of runners already asking for money. My friends came through with $1,200 for me to pass on to VASS.

I said hello to Gaynor Bourgeois while I was registering. Ultrarunning is a fairly small world, so wherever I'm running, I'm likely to find someone I've run with before. Gaynor had run in the Potomac Trail and Capon Valley 50Ks. We were both in the group that had gotten lost within 2 miles of the start at Potomac Trail. It was her first 100 too, and we were both hoping we'd stay on track this time.

I weighed in while I was at registration. During the race there are three medical checks (along with an additional voluntary check). At each one, runners are weighed to ensure that they haven't lost (due to dehydration) or gained (due to hyponatremia) a dangerous amount of weight. I was more afraid of losing too much weight and getting DQ'd, so I dressed light and left my water bottles at the hotel to minimize my starting weight. They weighed me in at 151 pounds.

I left registration and dropped by Jeff Washburn's trailer to say hi. Jeff is a member of Gil's Athletic Club (GAC), a trail running group in Topsfield, MA. We both belonged to an ultra mailing list, and Jeff had invited all the members to drop by if they were up in Vermont. He's a veteran of a number of ultras, so I picked his brain (and drank his root beer) before returning to town for lunch (pasta, of course).

Back at the motel, I figured it was time to quit dithering and decide which shoes I was going to wear. I had five pairs with me, two pairs of New Balance 706 trail shoes (one 2E width, one 4E), a pair of NB 827 road shoes, a pair of Nike Skylons, and the pair of NB 870 trail shoes that I'd bought on the way to Vermont.

From the course description, I knew that about 70 miles of the race was on dirt roads and jeep paths. The remainder was mostly mountain trails, with a few small sections on paved roads. It didn't seem like trail shoes were a necessity, and I wanted the additional cushioning of a road shoe. Unfortunately, I didn't have confidence in any of the shoes that I had with me. I'd been running in NB 828s and 827s for a long time, but New Balance had recently discontinued them, and I didn't like the replacement. My last pair of 827s was a bit too small, since my feet had spread some after all the training I'd been doing. I'd been having trouble finding tolerable replacements. The Skylons were the latest attempt, but I didn't have faith in them. I wasn't quite stupid enough to try the 870s for the first time in a 100-mile race, so I settled on the 2E 706s for the start. My crew would have the rest of the shoes with them. I could change to the road shoes when I started getting sore from the pounding or put on the 4E trail shoes if my feet swelled up.

After I finally made up my mind about the shoes, I rested until it was time to return to the start for the 4PM pre-race meeting. At the meeting, we went over the rules for crews. There were 33 aid stations along the course, where runners could pick up a variety of fluids, foods, or medical supplies. We were only allowed to meet with our crews at ten of the stations. Crews were supposed to follow specific routes to get to the stations to avoid runners and keep from annoying the locals.

A veteran ultramarathoner got up in front of the runners and treated us to a description of the course. It was not terribly useful. His 20-minute talk boiled down to telling us "and then you go up the hill, down, and then up again" over and over.

I skipped the pre-race dinner on the meadow and ate dinner in town so I'd be sure to be back at the hotel in time to meet with my crew. Mark and Karen were arriving that evening after they got out of work. They got to my hotel at about 7:30. We went over the plans for the next day and loaded their car with my gear and supplies. Then Mark and Karen went to Karen's parents' house in Claremont, NH to sleep.

I needed to get up at 2AM to get ready for the 4AM start. I set three alarm clocks (just in case), and then I took a sleeping pill. I was in bed and asleep by 10PM.

The first of the alarms woke me up at 2. I showered, dressed, and had a cup of coffee to wake up, with a PowerBar Harvest Bar and a few glasses of Gatorade to get me started on food and fluids. I started to eat a Slim Jim for some protein, but I didn't feel like finishing it. That was a portent of things to come.

I knew it was going to be a long run, so I put on body lube and nipple caps to reduce chafing. I knew I was going to hurt, so I had two ibuprophen, along with a Sudafed to clear my sinuses. I knew it was going to be hot, so I dressed in shorts and a singlet. I knew that while I ran, I was going to repeatedly clip the inside of my shins with the sole of the shoe on the opposite foot, so I wrapped some medical tape around my shins to keep them from getting scraped raw. I knew that I was likely to get blisters, especially on the ball of my right foot, so I coated that area with tincture of benzoin and stuck on a Compeed pad to protect it. I knew the pad wouldn't stick for 100 miles, but the longer I could keep from blistering, the better. Then I put on my socks and the trail shoes I'd picked, and at 3AM I left for the start.

It took about a half-hour to get to the dimly lit meadow. I parked and wandered over to the tent to wait for the start. It was more than warm enough already to hang out in just my running outfit, which didn't bode well for later in the day. More than 300 runners had registered. Some had already dropped out, but that left 241 runners, the horses and riders in the endurance ride, race officials, and all of their friends milling about waiting for the gun.

Just before 4AM the runners lined up in the field behind a banner that marked the starting line. The horses waited off to the side, since they weren't scheduled to start until an hour later. It was still before dawn, though there was a hint of light in the eastern sky. I went to the rear of the pack where I met Chris Martin, another ultra-list denizen I was seeing in the flesh for the first time. We chatted nervously for a few minutes, keeping an eye on our watches. At 4AM the waiting was over and we were off.

I was wearing a water bottle belt that held two 20-ounce bottles, along with a pouch that held the pills and assorted supplies I was carrying (electrolytes, ibuprofen, extra body lube, blister patches, wipes for toilet stops, etc...). I had two energy gel flasks, one in front in a belt clip and a spare stored in the pouch in back.

I was going to take a Succeed cap (electrolytes) and some carbohydrate gel every half hour, and two ibuprofen every third hour. I would drink some fluids whenever I took those, and whenever else I happened to think about drinking. I'd reload on fluids and snack on whatever food there was at the aid stations, and reload with pills and gel and get any gear I needed, like dry shoes and socks or lights for night running, from Mark and Karen at the stations where they were meeting me.

The race went according to plan for the first 40 miles. My plan was to walk up the hills and run the flats and downhills. I did the running sections at a "slow, comfortable pace" that started at about an 8:30-9 min./mile pace and slowed down some as I got tired and sore.

The hills were relentless, separated by very short "flat" sections. I was passing people while I was running, but many were passing me as we walked uphill. My walk was just my normal walk, and it wasn't as efficient at covering ground as that of everyone around me.

I expected that at these easy paces people would spend time running together and talking. There was some of that, but most of the time people weren't adjusting their pace to stay with other runners. I would talk with someone for a few minutes, as I (or they) slowly caught up and passed by. But as leisurely as it seemed, we were all racing, so we soon split and went on at our individual paces.

I don't remember exactly when my stomach started bothering me, but it was sometime early in the race. Whenever I looked at food, my stomach rebelled at the idea of eating any of it. I had a bit of peanut butter sandwich early and a bit of chicken and some soup later in the race, but that was nowhere near enough solid food to make up for the energy I was using. I had to depend on my gel and sports drinks for calories. The stomach problems may have been due to the coffee, the ibuprophen, not enough electrolytes, or something else. I never did solve them, but they never got really bad either. It was just one annoyance, and a minor one compared to the others that developed.

By the aid station at mile 45, I was almost 2 hours ahead of the pace for a 24-hour finish. But that was my peak as far as my time was concerned. By then, 20-plus miles of downhills had done a job on my quads. I was still running all the downhills and flats, but now there was considerable pain involved with each step.

Mark and Karen were waiting for me at the 45-mile aid station, and I decided to make my first shoe change. I thought that additional cushioning might help with the encroaching wear and tear, so I went to the NB 827s. This turned out to be a mistake. The shoes were already a bit short, and my feet had swollen over the previous 45 miles. So my toes, especially the two big toes, took a beating over the next 11 miles, until I met my crew again at the aid station at mile 56.

At that station I sat down to rest for the first time, instead of just reloading and plugging on. It was past 2PM, and the heat of the day had taken a toll on me on top of all the miles. It was up in the 80s at times, awfully warm for running long distances. The shade from the trees helped, and I heard that thunderstorms had cooled some of the runners. Unfortunately, I never saw more than a few sprinkles and leftover puddles.

Fifty-six miles into the race, I was hot, tired, sweaty, and covered with bugs. Thoughts of dropping out began to enter my mind. My time for the 11 miles from the previous crew station had slowed behind the 24-hour pace. I was still almost two hours ahead of that pace overall, but between the pain and my reduced speed, it was obvious that the second half of the race wasn't going to go as well as I had hoped. I knew that I could keep going, but the remaining 45 miles seemed like an awful long way, especially considering how I already felt.

While I was sitting there, my left adductor began to cramp up. I thought that might be a sign that I needed more electrolytes, so I decided to take two Succeed caps every half hour and see if that helped.

Mark was talking about running along with me for few miles later in the day, starting at about 68 miles, blissfully unaware of my doubts at this point. I decided I would get going and reassess how I was doing the next time I saw my crew, which would be about five miles farther along. First, I changed into the Skylons. I still wasn't confident in them, but I knew that at least they were longer, so I'd have more toe room. Then I continued on.

It was uphill leaving the station, so I was walking when a couple of horses passed me. One of the riders had done the race before, and he told me to look forward to the view at the end of the climb. I immediately focused on the important word there – "climb" – and began to worry. It turned out that the entire three miles to the next aid station was uphill, with no shade, in the worst heat of the day. The aid station at the top was unmanned, so there wasn't even anyone there to cheer me up. The view was wonderful, but I couldn't care less.

A couple of uncomfortable downhill miles later, running on what were by now quadburgers, I met my crew again at the 60-mile aid station. My feet were even more uncomfortable in the Skylons, as impossible as that seemed, so I made what turned out to be my final shoe change, to the 4E NB706s.

I also had my face wiped by Jim Gilford, one of the GAC crew. Jim is the "Gil" of the GAC, a familiar figure at races, but I didn't learn that until later. Much earlier in the race, I'd seen him wiping off GAC runners with a terrycloth mitt soaked in ice water. I knew how good that felt from the finish of the San Diego marathon, so I asked if I could try it. He didn't have time then, but he remembered me asking and when he saw me again, he had time to wipe me down. This was about 5:30PM. The heat of the day was fading away, and the cool, clean feeling from the ice water wash was incredible, so I found the energy to plod on.

By now, my pauses to rest at the stations where Mark and Karen were waiting for me with a chair were stretching to 15 minutes. All day long they had everything ready so I could rush through the aid station if I wanted to, but the further I got into the race, the better the option of sitting awhile seemed. The rest didn't really allow for much recovery, but it still helped some physically. Of course, the longer I rested, the more time I had for internal discussion while I sat there panting (in spite of the slow pace) and staring off into space. I was still struggling with doubts, but I broke it down. A little over eight miles to the next crew station. That seemed do-able. Then another 8 miles with Mark, which would be a change from running by myself. Then there'd only be about 23 miles to go. None of that seemed impossible when I broke it down that way, just not very pleasant. As long as I didn't think too much about the number of miles I'd already come. Oh well, on we go.

Another 8 miles of up and down. Time was passing fairly quickly, though the miles were not. I was getting a little sloppy with the half-hourly consumption of gel and electrolytes. The effort to keep going was taking up more of my attention, so I missed a few. Still, when the medical team checked, my weight was good, so I assumed I was doing OK.

Somewhere along this section, I met up with Gaynor Bourgeois again. That sparked my competitiveness a little. We went back and forth, passing each other through a long downhill stretch, until I led her into the crew station at mile 69, still about an hour ahead of 24-hour pace. Here I had another rest, another internal dialog, and some soup. Eating still wasn't appealing, and the idea of dry food was nauseating, but a little soup was better than nothing.

Some of the other runners were picking up their pacers at this station. The pacers would run with them for the last 31 miles. I hadn't arranged for a pacer, but after running almost 70 miles, I could see how assistance and moral support from someone with a clear mind could help.

It was getting towards dusk, so I put on my headlamp and packed a spare hand light and some extra batteries in the pouch in my belt. When I took off, Mark came along. He was running the next eight miles with me to the next crew station. We left about the same time as Gaynor, and we all walked together up a long stretch of rough trail. When we reached the top and started running again, Gaynor pulled away.

The course continued rolling up and down along the edge of some woods. Where the trail curved under the trees, we were running in the dark. Mark and I turned on our lights so we could see. Soon we needed our lights the whole time.

By now, I was walking the uphills, and then walking on after the peak of the hill to look at the downhill section before I began to run again. Each downhill step was tearing a bit more out of my quads, muscle fiber that I didn't have to spare. I was sneaking in more and more walking at the bottom of the hills and along what little level course there was. I went a little faster with Mark along than I might have otherwise, but I still slowed down dramatically during this leg of the race. The last horse in the field caught up and passed me during this time.

We reached a pleasantly soft horse trail and began climbing steadily again. By now it was completely dark. As we went along, moths bombarded my light. Since the light was strapped to my head, the moths were incredibly annoying. Mark had a hand light, and we could see that the moths weren't attacking his light nearly as much. We figured that it was probably because his light was dimmer. The course was marked with glow sticks in addition to the yellow plates used during the day, so I only needed my light to see the footing. At my current pace, I didn't need a bright light for that, so I turned my headlamp down and that helped with the moth problem.

When we finally reached the next handlers' station at about 77 miles, I was still a few minutes ahead of 24-hour pace, but I was pretty much done. The thoughts of dropping out were much louder now, and their arguments were better. I sat down to rest, and soon I started to shiver. Karen went and got me a shirt, but I figured I'd warm back up when (if) I started up again, and changing seemed like a lot of work, so I didn't put it on at first.

I got up to think about proceeding, but I found that my legs had stiffened up while I sat. I staggered around for a few steps and then I sat again. I tried getting up a few more times, but I didn't get more than a few paces from the chair.

I didn't know if I was going to continue, but if I went on, clearly there'd be little, if any, running. Walking 23 miles when I was already beat was not something I was looking forward to at all. I was still shivering. Fuzzily, I realized that whether or not I went on, I'd want the shirt. Also, putting it on was another way to stall before I had to decide what to do.

My internal debate was pretty obvious to my external observers. Mark said that he and Karen weren't going to be the ones to say I should quit. That didn't help much. I kept the debate going while I stumbled around more, and then Mark said something that did help. He told me that anyone could sign up for a race, but that the glory went to those who finished. That was trite, but it was enough to inspire me to make up my mind to keep going, in spite of the long, tedious effort continuing would require.

So I left. Unfortunately, the route through the aid station and back on the course led gently downhill, and I found it most uncomfortable. As I weaved through the crowd at the station, I listed a bit to one side and then the other. A few people asked if I needed anything with a "he doesn't look so good" look on their faces, but they didn't have any spare legs on hand, and my responses seemed coherent enough, so they let me go on.

After I walked some, I loosened up a tiny bit and settled into a steady pace. I could still climb the hills about as well as I had been doing, but I was reduced to an uncomfortable semi-stagger going downhill. I tried running a few times on the flatter parts of the course, but I went no more than a few steps before I gave up on that idea.

It was a very long, lonely 12-mile walk through the night on almost totally empty roads and trails, broken up a couple of times by aid stations and a couple of times as someone went by. There didn't seem like there was any danger that I'd collapse, but I definitely wasn't catching anyone! A runner named Vince Devlin passed me during that time. We were both walking, but he was walking a little faster. However, every time we reached an aid station he stayed a little longer that I did, so he'd have to pass me again. We kept exchanging positions for the rest of the race. Going back and forth with him helped keep me going.

Vince stuck with me to talk a little before we reached the crew station at 89 miles, but as we approached the barn where the station was located, he pulled ahead again. The last medical check was at this station. Mark was there, sitting alone in a chair. I said "hi" to him as I went to the scale but he was zoned out and didn't notice me. Karen was napping in their car. It had been a very long day for them too.

I had stayed within two pounds of my starting weight at all of the medical checks, and I was still at a good weight at this one even though I'd pretty much stopped taking my electrolytes. I figured I wasn't sweating that much while I was walking in the dark, so I didn't need them. That was not a good decision, but by now I was totally focused on finishing, with little spare capacity left for rational thought.

My feet had begun to blister uncomfortably in a few spots, so I slowly took off my shoes, emptied out some trail crud, and put them back on, hoping that'd help. It was a challenging task, but emptying my shoes did allow me to sneak in some sitting time before I moved on.

I left the station and was soon slogging along alone. Somewhere along the way I had stopped thinking about dropping out. I knew I could make it to the finish if I could find the patience to keep going at my glacial pace, so I was looking for ways to mentally frame the remaining part of the race to make it palatable. I had a little less than 11 miles to go, and that distance was broken up by three aid stations, including one more crew station at mile 95. The next aid station was three miles away. I was used to taking 20 minutes to race that distance. Today it would take me an hour, more or less, to travel those three miles. At best, the finish was over three hours away, but I was trying not to think that far ahead. I knew if I just kept drifting along, the time and miles would pass by at their own rate and eventually drop me off at the finish.

I was lost in my thoughts when I was startled by something jumping at me out of the corner of my eye. I stopped and turned my head to point my light at whatever it was, but all I could see were some bushes. So I started walking – and there it was again! This happened a few more times and I started to work myself into a panic. I began to walk faster, keeping my head turned while I was moving so I could watch for whatever it was that was stalking me. That's when I realized that all I was seeing was the shadows of the bushes moving as my headlamp bobbed up and down. I calmed down and moved on.

It was still dark when Jeff Washburn passed me. His slow, steady trot demonstrated once again that pacing is the key to success.

Dawn broke. That helped my head clear some. I picked up the pace a little and found some company temporarily when I managed to slowly pass a woman and her pacer on a climb. That little success felt good. I hope that they enjoyed it just as much when, soon afterwards, they passed me back and left me behind.

I reached the top of another hill, and there was a woman standing there, directing us to take a left turn to go to the next aid station. I was glad to see her. Normally, there weren't people out on the course directing traffic so I assumed her presence meant that the aid station was nearby. As I passed her, I joked that I must still have to go over another mountain to get to the station. Unfortunately, that was true. Given that what little brainpower I had left was totally consumed in generating Relentless Forward Motion, when the time that I thought it "should" take to get to the next station had passed, I began to get anxious. I managed to convince myself that I must be lost, even though I was regularly passing course markers. So I stopped, and yelled "hello" a few times, looking for help. Luckily, another runner came along and got me moving forward again before I did anything too stupid.

I reached the crew station at mile 95, where Mark and Karen were waiting. We were all eager to get this over with and get some real rest, so I dropped my light and visor off with them and headed right back out again.

A mile or two into my latest stroll, I noticed that my hands and fingers had swollen and turned a dark purplish color out as far as the middle knuckle. My fingertips were still quite pale. I knew somewhere in the back of my head that there was something that I could do about that, but it wasn't popping up, so I admired the evidence that what I was doing was difficult enough to cause mysterious physical issues, and wandered on.

Vince passed me one last time, and then I remembered. Edema (swelling) in extremities = not enough electrolytes, and I hadn't been taking my capsules. I took a couple of Succeed caps, and luckily, I was right. The extra electrolytes helped quickly. The next time I thought to check my hands, the swelling had disappeared.

I passed the last (unmanned) aid station, which meant there was only 2.1 miles to go. There weren't any real mountains left, but there was some dirt trail. The horses had churned it up pretty well, which made the footing a little treacherous. I would have liked to have been there earlier, on pace for a 24-hour finish, but I was glad that I wasn't trying to run it in the dark.

After that, there was a loop through a meadow. The open space was large enough to let me see some other runners. Vince Devlin was still in sight, though he continued to pull away. Ray Mount was staggering so badly that I knew I'd pass him. However, while I was reeling him in, I was passed by a runner and his pacer who were jogging along happily, chatting, and looking way too fresh to be in the same race as the rest of us. Good for them, I thought, but if they could still run that well, what were they doing back here with me?

There was someone waiting at the end of the meadow, where we got back onto forest trail. I was close enough to the pair who were still running to hear them ask him how far it was to the finish. He told them 10 minutes walking, or four at their pace. It ended up being closer to 15 minutes for me, after some bizarre twists in the trail that must have been added just to bug me, but finally I could see the banner at the finish through a gap in the trees. The ground was soft enough, and I found I still had a little adrenaline left to give me a lift. I managed to run the last 20 yards or so, and I was done!

My time of 27:29:24 put me in 134th place. I wasn't even the first Charbonneau to finish, but I made it, something that a third of the starters didn't do. I had started running with a time in the back of my mind, but I ended just happy to survive. The last 23 miles had taken over 9 hours. On this day, that was fast enough for me.

I lost the race by over 12 hours. The winner finished his race the previous day, in just under 15 hours. He was from Massachusetts, but to me he was a Kenyan. Anyone who was running to win was running in an entirely different race from me.

It was quiet at the finish at 7:30 in the morning. A few of the faster runners were waiting there, wrapped in blankets, applauding as others straggled in. I actually made it to the finish a little before Mark and Karen. Due to my confusion in the woods while I was finding my way to mile 95, it appeared like I was slowing down, so they didn't rush to meet me. But they arrived soon after I did, took some pictures, and shared in the joy and relief.

I was toast. It would have been nice to hang around and socialize, and maybe stay for brunch and the awards ceremony, but the idea of lying down on my motel room bed was just too appealing. Mark and Karen were ready to take me back and drop me off so they could get some sleep, but I made them wait while I took advantage of the free massage in the medical tent. I apologized to Mark for the delay, and I explained that I could never turn down a massage from a young, pretty girl. He gave me an odd look, and later there was photographic evidence that indicated my judgment might have been impaired at the time.

We got into the car and drove back to the motel. Mark and Karen unloaded my gear. All weekend long, they had been the foundation upon which everything rested. Mark and Karen were always at the crew stations on time waiting for me, not an easy task on the indirect routes on unmarked roads that they had to use to avoid the runners. Everything I needed that was possible to get was provided cheerfully. They were familiar faces in an intimidating new environment, encouraging without being saccharine. It was time to say goodbye, but I was sad to see them go.

I went in my room and fell down on the bed. Sleep would have been nice, but dozing was the best I could do. I was so sore that any movement woke me up again.

After a while I got up, showered, and assessed the damage. There was some chafing and a few blisters, but nothing so bad that it really affected my race. My feet were battered, but I had expected that. I was going to lose the nails on both big toes. The right toenail angled up in the air, supported by an enormous blister that I had to be drain before I could put my shoes on again. My kneecaps were both tender and sore. My quads were the worst. For the next few days, every time I stood up, I had to wobble for a minute before I loosened up enough to be sure I wouldn't fall down.

By Tuesday, the worst of that was over. My quads, along with my knees and feet, were still a little sore, but I was on my way to recovering.

I considered my race a success. I didn't buckle, but I did finish, after a mighty struggle. It was probably too soon to worry about whether I would try again, but I already knew in the back of my mind that I would.

Ruth and I with our wedding party at the 2008 Kerouac 5K

Chapter 10: Maybe a Little Too Far

"I often start out running with the wind at my back. So I feel good and I keep running a little farther, forgetting that it will be in my face on the way home."
                    - Jim Sweeney

In the 2004 Vermont 100, I finally discovered the answer to a question I'd been asking myself for some time: I found out how far I could go before I couldn't run any farther. The answer was about 77 miles, if I was running on an extremely challenging course. Then I somehow found a way to push through that barrier and keep going until I reached the finish line.

Finishing the Vermont 100 was a peak experience. The race left me feeling more successful and confident than ever before. I had to abuse my body to get that feeling, but that's what addicts do. I thought it was worth it, and like any other junkie, I wanted more.

Even before I recovered enough so I could walk normally, I started planning for another try. This time just finishing wouldn't be enough. I wanted to finish in less than 24 hours and earn my buckle. To do that, I needed to cut three-and-a-half hours off my time. I looked back on my race to figure out what I had learned and how I could use that to improve.

The simplest way for me to finish faster would be to run farther. The last 23 miles had taken nine hours, so there was plenty of room for improvement there.

I was doing my extra-long runs every three or four weeks, whenever I could find a convenient long race. That made my training schedule somewhat haphazard, but eliminated the boredom of running 30 or 40 miles all by myself. This had worked pretty well so far. I planned to keep the same loose structure for my long runs while looking for ways to put in even more miles.

More mileage would help, but I wasn't sure I had really exhausted my endurance in Vermont. The main reason I had to stop running after 77 miles was that my quadriceps were so painful I couldn't keep running. Downhill running did the most damage. The more tired I got, the more I leaned back and coasted down hills without worrying about my form. I was landing on my heels and braking with every step. If I could avoid that, I'd reduce the wear and tear on my quads.

I had access to a gym at work, and I started going regularly to add some weight work. I figured if I had stronger quads and core trunk muscles, they would help me endure the abuse and hold better form further into the race.

In addition to training harder, there were a number of things that I thought I could try during the race to help my time.

I admire purists who try to do these races without a crew, but I would have been lost without mine. I needed someone to manage my gear and keep me on track. Sharing the experience with Mark and Karen had made all of it better. I decided to try to find a pacer to add to my crew. A good pacer might be able to lead me along a little faster through the last 30 miles. One would certainly help me get through the times where I'm confused because of exhaustion and lack of sleep. But he (or she) had to be the right person so the chemistry would work. My pacer would be spending more time with me than the rest of the crew, possibly in dire circumstances.

The old adage, "start slow, then ease off" definitely applies to ultramarathoning. If I ran slower at the start of the race, I could keep close to my initial pace, whatever it is, further into the race. As long as I can hold my pace in an ultra, sooner or later I begin to pass people. Each time I slowly reel in another runner, I get a little lift that helps me get to the next person. It takes a long time to pass someone at my pace, but that gives me something to do besides think about my discomfort.

Getting through the aid stations faster could easily save a big chunk of time. I learned a new phrase from the GAC runners in Vermont: "Beware the chair." I spent well over an hour, maybe as much as two hours, sitting, resting, and gathering the determination to move on. Getting out of the chair and moving again got harder after every break. I don't know how much the rest helped keep me going. Sitting less during the race might end up hurting me towards the end. Still, I was sure that I could spend less time in the chair.

The summer heat was a problem. The terrycloth mitt soaked in icewater that GAC had for their runners would be a great addition to my crew's kit. A small cloth bag for ice to go under my hat when it's hottest would be another useful thing. We tried a plastic sandwich bag, but it didn't help much. A cloth bag that slowly lets some icewater leak out would work much better.

I also needed to take enough electrolytes to replace the ones I sweated away. I got stupid as the race went on. If I set my watch to beep every half-hour, that would make it simpler to remember when it was time to take the Suceed capsules.

I wasn't able to eat real food during most of the race. Energy gels and carbohydrate drinks provided enough energy, but some extra protein and fats from food might have helped extend the useful life of my quads. I decided to try training with liquid food substitutes like Ensure to see whether I could use them during a race to get more nutrients.

The chafing and blistering after 100 miles wasn't too bad. I did a pretty good job of protecting myself from friction, but I knew some of that was luck. I was dry through most of the race, except for sweat. If the weather had been worse, friction from wet gear would have been much more of a problem.

Using different shoe models during the race to change the inevitable friction points between the shoes and my feet worked well. It was also good to have a slightly larger pair of shoes for later in the race. Softer shoes might have helped some with the pounding. Running in a pair of shoes that didn't fit right was just dumb, but at least I resisted the temptation to run in my new trail shoes.

If I started to lose the ability to run downhill again, I could try running the uphill sections instead of walking. Running would be harder work, but it had to be faster than walking, and running uphill would put less stress on my quads.

The one most important thing I had learned was how difficult it was just to finish a 100-mile race. Low spots were unavoidable. I hoped my experience would help me be better prepared for them, and hopefully help me get through the low spots fast enough to buckle next time.

So far my ultramarathon efforts had paid off with fun and success, so I was eager to get started on the next round. I decided I'd go back to Vermont. There were other 100-mile races I could try, but I figured they could wait. It would be hard enough to go back to Vermont and try to do better without adding more travel and a different course to the problem. That meant I had a year to get ready for the next race.

Two weeks after the Vermont 100 I felt like I had recovered enough to start to ramp up my training again. I put in a 30-mile week and everything felt fine, except for a little pain in my left hip. I did my first post-race long run three weeks after the race, a 28-mile run around Lake Quannapowitt, in the mid-August heat on concrete and asphalt, at the 24 Hour Relay. That irritated my hip a little more, but I ignored it.

I ran 22 miles on the Saturday of Labor Day weekend, and then I followed that up on Labor Day by winning my age group in the Malden Irish-American 5K in 20:14. It wasn't a particularly fast time, but the faster runners were all doing the 10K. I celebrated my medal with copious amounts of free post-race beer.

The next weekend, I tried a new way to extend my long run. I was already doing more than 40 miles at a time on some training runs. That was fine when I was preparing for 50-mile races, but I wanted more to get ready for the 100s. Extending my weekend training runs to 50 or 60 miles would help, but there were multiple problems with that idea. There were very few races of that length available to me that I could use for training runs. Running for 12-15 hours all by myself wouldn't be fun. It would require mental toughness that I wasn't sure I had. And longer runs would use up the entire day and probably require a significant amount of recovery time afterwards, at least at first.

Instead of trying to get all the miles into one run, I decided to break them up into two runs. On Saturday, I ran 30 miles using the 5-to-1 run-to-walk ratio I used for my longest training runs. Then on Sunday, I ran another 19, this time without walking so I could run along with some friends from SRR while they were doing their own long runs. I was still tired from Saturday while I was running on Sunday, so I got to practice what it felt like to run deep into an ultra, but by breaking the run up I didn't get worn down as much. That meant I didn't have to interrupt my training significantly while I recovered.

That plan worked well enough so that two weekends later I was able to race leg 4 of the Lake Winnipesaukee Relay with a SRR team on Saturday and then run the 50K at the Vermont 50 on Sunday.

The weather in Vermont couldn't have been more different from what it had been the previous year. Instead of a downpour, we enjoyed a beautiful New England fall weekend, with blue skies and a warm sun bringing out the peak colors of the foliage.

The 50K shares most of its course with the 50-mile race. It included the section I got lost on in 2003. This time, I had no problem staying on track, and my sore hip felt better running on trails instead of roads. I finished the race in 5:49. Once again, running the day's lesser race paid off. I went home with a plaque for finishing third in my age group.

Three weeks later, I was back in Vermont for the Green Mountain Marathon. I spent three days prior to the race in bed with a fever, but I felt better on race day so I went to the start to get in a training run.

The race is run on a pleasant out-and-back course on quiet roads along the northern shores of Lake Champlain. I had run part of the course before, in a half-marathon that they used to hold at the same time as the marathon. The main feature that I remembered from the half was the cold wind from Canada that blows off the lake and across the course year after year.

This year there was early sun, the wind was subdued, and I cruised through the first half of the race at a pace well under my Boston qualifying time. In the second half of the race the sun went behind the clouds, the cold wind swept in, and my sore hip acted up. I slowed down dramatically and finished in 3:36.

After the marathon I had four weeks to get ready for my next big challenge, the Stone Cat 50. Jeff Washburn of Gil's Athletic Club, whom I had met in Vermont, was the race director. GAC holds the Stone Cat on a 12.5-mile loop of trail in Ipswich, MA. The 50-mile runners do four loops, while other runners stop after two loops (plus a little more) to make a marathon.

My sore hip persisted through two more weeks of training. I needed to take some time to let it get better, but I didn't want to skip the 50 and miss the chance to get in a long training run in a race that was a short drive from home. That weekend, GAC was organizing a practice run on the Stone Cat course. I decided to grind through that and then shut things down until the race, where I'd take my chances and see how my hip held up. The training run went OK. Afterwards, for the next two weeks, I didn't run any more than three to five miles a day.

The first snowstorm of the year arrived on race day. The race was scheduled to start at 6AM so most of us would finish before dark, but the snow took down a utility pole on the road to the start, so traffic had to be redirected. Jeff delayed the start of the race for an hour while everyone found the new route to the starting line, which was next to a school on the edge of the Willowdale State Forest.

I was worried about finding the trail in the snow, but when we finally got going, I had no problems. The path was clearly marked by the footprints of the runners ahead of me.

At the end of each loop, I could duck back into the school at the start for a break and to restock my personal supplies. There were also two aid stations on the course, manned by cheerful GAC members serving hot soup and drinks. As the day passed, the GACers at the aid stations got more cheerful as they drained their stock of beer. I held off on sampling the brew while I was running. The aid crews looked like they needed what they had to ward off the cold, and there was the promise of beer for the runners at the finish.

The mix of snow and runners made for ever-changing trail conditions throughout the day. On the first loop, I churned through the snowy tracks left by the marathoners and 50 milers ahead of me. The second time around, the snow had slacked off and the trail was hard-packed and slippery. By the third pass, the snow was worn down and I was running on rocks and mud, but by the fourth loop the marathoners and faster ultrarunners were long gone, the snow had picked up again, and there was plenty of loose snow to soften the trail. My hip never bothered me while I was running. I finished after dark in a time of 9:51.

After the experience of finishing a 100-mile race, running a 50-mile race was much less daunting. I was much more confident while I was running. In spite of the weather, I knew I was going to finish. I treated it as a training run and didn't go all out, but I was still pleased with my time. My only issue was that there was no beer left when I was done, but Jeff shared some of his personal stash of root beer with me before I left for home.

I did two weeks of light running to recover, and then it was time to run the Mill Cities Relay with my SRR teammates. I ran the last two legs at Mill Cities, about 14 miles. My hip still felt fine, so I got back on track with my training for Vermont.

The rest of my life wasn't going as well as my running. My wife and I were drifting apart. I spent more time away from the house. Bars, hashes, and long runs helped me avoid doing any work to keep my marriage together. We ended up splitting late in 2004 and getting a divorce early in 2005.

I started doing more socializing with a beer in my hand at hashes and pub runs. I drank to excess at times, but I managed my binges to avoid interfering with my long runs. I was in good enough shape so I could do quite a bit of drinking and still get in most of my runs.

I had a good job managing computer systems, but I wasn't invested in it anymore. My work was easy, it fit in with my running schedule, there was some travel that took me to new places to run, and the pay and benefits were better than anything else I was likely to find, but that wasn't enough. Maybe it's a cliché, but if I had to show up to work every day, I wanted to do something that made me happy. Unfortunately, I had no idea what that might be.

In retrospect, it's hard to tell how much my running contributed to my difficulties. The running was the only part of my life that I found rewarding. In true addictive fashion, instead of cutting back on my running to work on my problems, I increased the dosage, at least in part to try to avoid them. My accomplishments and the recognition they earned made me feel good, so I pushed even further to get more of that good feeling.

I was asking running to carry an awful lot of weight, especially for what was essentially a frivolous pursuit. I was never going to be a good enough to make a living at running. Letting it take over my life was not a long-term solution. But in the short term, I was still grabbing for more and it was paying off.

I wanted to get in more of my long runs on trails, so in January I began to drive to Topsfield on Sundays for long runs with GAC. Their runs were typically on trails through the local parks and forests. I had usually avoided driving to training runs before, starting all my runs from my front door with few exceptions. Using a car to run just seemed wasteful. But now that I wanted more, every Sunday I drove about 30 miles to Jim Gilford's store (he's the "Gil" in GAC) in Topsfield to meet with the group for a run.

There were a lot of experienced ultrarunners in GAC, so I was able to learn from their stories. My own training and goals didn't seem unusual to them. After the run, we retired to the store basement. Gilly kept a keg of beer there so we recovered with beer, poker, and conversation.

Then I would drive into Boston to run a few more miles and drink more beer with the Boston Hash. Most Sundays, that was all I'd do – run and drink.

It was now 2005, and I only had half a year left to finish getting ready for Vermont. I began to pile on the long runs. On Jan. 8, I ran the GAC Fat Ass 50K in 5:24. Three weeks later, I ran 35 miles by myself on Saturday and 17 on Sunday with Boston's L Street marathon training group. A week after that, I ran the 16-mile Boston Prep race in Derry, and the following weekend I ran 17 miles on Saturday and 19 (and a hash) on Sunday.

Three more 20-mile runs, and then in mid-March I left the New England snow behind and flew to Virginia on a business trip. That weekend I drove my rental car to Maryland. There, I met up with a group from GAC that had driven a van down from Massachusetts, and we ran the HAT Run 50K. I had a great run in the pleasant spring weather, saw some deer along the trail, and finished in 4:56 without any undue strain.

I had one more big effort planned before Vermont. Back in January, registration opened for the Bull Run 50-Mile Race. I had to decide whether I was going to enter so I could get in before the race filled up. I needed the race as a training run, and I could arrange my business travel to put me in Virginia that week. But Bull Run was the week before Boston, and I wanted to keep my streak of consecutive Boston Marathons going. I decided to enter both races and see how that worked out. I wouldn't run either race *fast*, but it's not like I was going to win either of them anyhow.

So on Saturday, April 9th, I drove from DC to Clifton, VA, for the Bull Run. It was a sunny 70 degrees and the early spring trees didn't provide much shade, so I finished with a bit of a sunburn. My time of 9:49 was a new 50-mile PR. That was pleasant, but since there were no mountains, mud, or snow on the course, and long trail races aren't measured all that accurately anyhow, I didn't make too much out of shaving two minutes off my PR. I didn't have any problems that would keep me from running Boston.

I didn't want to just sit in my hotel after the race. There wasn't much to do in the area, but there's always a bar around, so I went out for a beer that night. The bar was empty, so I only stayed for one beer, but my legs were sore from the race so I was staggering when I walked out of the bar. That attracted the attention of a cop who must have figured from the way I was walking that I was drunk. He followed me to my car in his cruiser, and then trailed me as I drove very carefully back to my hotel.

I took a few days off to recover, and then I ran 4 miles at Khoury's on Thursday night, followed by a few beers to get me ready for a weekend of pre-marathon hashing. Every year the Boston hash puts on a weekend-long celebration as a counterweight to Patriot Day's big race. I joined in for Friday night's pub crawl, and then I ran the 6 miles of the official Marathon Hash on Saturday, with copious beer during and after the run.

On Sunday, I skipped the hash activities and went to the marathon expo to pick up my number. At the expo, I stopped by the Saucony booth to check out the three-foot poster of myself hanging on their wall. Saucony was running an ad campaign at major races called the "Sacuony 26". They picked 26 runners with interesting stories to represent the company, one for each mile. Many of the stories involved running with injuries or illnesses, but they found my story of running a 50 the week before Boston interesting enough to include me in the group. For participating, I got a complete Saucony running outfit, which I had to wear during the race, $10 per mile, which I planned on donating to the Vermont 100 charity, and entry for me and a guest to a post-race party at a bar overlooking the finish line.

Marathon Monday was a nice day for a run. The sun came out as the day went on, but it never got too hot. I was busy with ultramarathoning so I hadn't qualified, which meant I was running with one of the numbers the BAA gives to SRR for helping out at their events. That meant I started in the back of the pack with the charity runners and other non-qualifiers. I was so far back that it took me over 20 minutes to reach the starting line after the gun went off.

It was a good thing that I wasn't trying to race. Because of my starting position I spent the whole race weaving through crowds of slower runners. I kept the spirit of the hash weekend going with a few beer breaks along the way. My first beer was at about mile 6, when I stopped in the Happy Swallow in Framingham. The patrons there bought me a beer and took a few pictures. The next day, the Framingham paper mentioned me as "the mystery runner" in a brief note in their marathon story. My next beer was at mile 20, where the Boston hash has their beer check. It's like a water stop, only they hand out beer to anyone who wants some, instead of water. I had one more beer before the finish, from a can donated by a spectator at mile 21, near Boston College.

The running itself was uneventful. At the pace I was going, I felt no ill effects from the previous weekend's 50 miler. As I approached the finish line, I caught up with Gilly, who was continuing his yearly tradition of running Boston as a "bandit," and we crossed the finish line together with the clock reading 4:10. My chip time, which didn't include the time lost at the start, was 3:48.

I stopped by the Saucony party at the finish line, where I had a couple more beers. I picked up my poster from the expo booth for a memento. Then I headed over to a nearby pub for the hash post-marathon/post-weekend party and one more beer, but by that point we were all ready to wind things up for the weekend.

My poster and I rode home on the bus. I was tired but happy with the results of my experiment. Both the Bull Run and Boston had gone well, and my confidence was sky-high. I was dreaming about bigger things that I'd heard about from my friends at GAC and on the Internet – running some of the other major ultras like Western States or Hardrock, or maybe even moving up to harder challenges, like the Grand Slam (four mountain 100s – Vermont, Western States, Leadville, and Wasatch Front - in a single year) or Coyote4Play (a weekend of multiple 40 mile+ runs, mixed in with beer, bowling, and other foolishness).

But first, I had to finish getting ready for Vermont. In early May, I ran 33 miles at the GAC Mother's Day 6 Hour. On Memorial Day weekend, I ran 11 miles with my friend Mark on Saturday, participated in the Burlington hash's marathon pub crawl that night, ran from my hotel to the start of the Vermont City Marathon the next morning, ran the marathon in 3:35 (including a short stop at the mile 23 beer check), had a beer at the post-race festival and ran back to my hotel, and ran the marathon hash later that afternoon, for a total of 33 miles on Sunday.

June 5 was the Nipmuck Trail Marathon in Connecticut. I carpooled down with a group from GAC. The advertising for the race says, "If you don't have health insurance don't do this race. No matter how careful you are, plan on falling." They were right. I've seen plenty of runners hit the wall in a marathon, but Nipmuck was the only race I've been in where I saw another runner crash headfirst into a tree. It was a hot day, and I ran my slowest marathon ever, a 5:47, but I had to sit and shiver for 20 minutes after the race before I could get up and walk around.

After Nipmuck, I felt invincible. I thought I was ready to do great things in Vermont, relative to my personal scale for success. I wasn't expecting to win, of course, but I was now expecting to meet my goal of finishing Vermont in less than 24 hours. But as most models of addiction show, this feeling of confidence is just the prelude to a crash.

Between all the long runs, I was jumping into shorter races to spend some time with my SRR friends. On June 12, I ran the Battle of Bunker Hill 8K on a hot day in Charlestown. My back was sore afterwards, but that wasn't unusual. I sat down on the ground to talk for a while. When I stood up, it felt like someone had jabbed a knife in my lower back. Hunching over helped some, but the pain returned every time I tried to straighten up.

I grabbed some ice from a nearby cooler and applied it to my back. The pain ebbed after a while, and I was able to stand up and walk around without wincing. A day later, I continued my training, but now it seemed like there was a little extra heaviness to my legs. That was where my certainty that I could run forever began to erode.

I had one last long run scheduled before Vermont. Every year, Joe Hayes organizes a training run on Mt. Agamenticus in York, ME. The course is a 3-mile loop that goes up and down the mountain, an abandoned ski area. Joe holds the run on the same day as Western States, which was on June 25 in 2005.

I rode up with Jeff Washburn and some others from GAC. It was another hot and sunny day. The uphill portion of the trail was in the open on flat rocks, and the sun turned the rocks into a frying pan. The rest of the course was nice and shady, heading downhill on a dirt trail, and then looping around the base of the mountain on a road to get back to the climb. I planned on doing ten loops, but I stopped after nine, telling myself that in the heat, and with only three weeks before Vermont, that was more than enough.

The next day was one last race, the POW-MIA 10K in South Boston. My time on the flat course was only 45:02, but it was another extremely hot day, so I blamed the weather and put the race behind me to start tapering for Vermont.

I had enjoyed the last year of training in large part because I had a lot of success without a lot of pre-race stress, since I was treating every race like just another training run. But it seemed like instead of avoiding stress, I had just been saving it all up for now. Sometimes I can enjoy the break from training while I taper, but when it's an important race, it's hard for me to manage my tension without the release of running. I had gone through this before with marathons while trying to qualify for Boston, but this time the potential reward and the associated risk were much larger. I wasn't sleeping well, my legs felt tired, and I worried that I wasn't recovering well enough to be fresh on race day.

I drove to Vermont for the race. I hadn't been able to get a room at the hotel I stayed at in 2004, and that took a little more from my comfort level. At race registration, I turned in the money I'd collected for VASS, about half of what I had collected in 2004. I returned to my hotel, skipping most of the pre-race activities in a last-ditch effort to rest before the race.

My attitude going into the race was dramatically different from the previous year. In 2004 I wanted to finish, but I wasn't afraid of failing. Mostly, I was curious. I was there to find out what I could do. For 2005, I had done a lot more preparation, Mark and Karen were there to crew for me again, and I had Gilly lined up to pace me through the last 30 miles. I knew the race would be hard, and I was anxious about failing. I felt that if I didn't buckle, I would have wasted all my work and let my friends down. By this point, my faith in my training had almost disappeared. A feeling of dread hovered over everything, and I just wanted to get the race over with.

My memories of race day are mostly a blur. At the start, it was uncomfortably warm and sticky. Soon after dawn, the temperatures rose well into the 80s, another in a long string of hot and humid days. I should have adjusted my plan and walked a lot more during the day to take it easy. Then, if I made it through the day, I could have made an attempt to make up time towards buckling at night. Instead, I stubbornly went ahead with my original plan, in the blind hope that things would work out. The results were not good.

In 2004, I averaged about 12 minutes per mile for more than 50 miles before I began to slow down. In 2005, by the time I reached 30 miles I had already fallen off pace. My back hurt, my hamstrings hurt, and I was throwing up every time I tried to eat anything. Even the liquid food substitute I had trained with wasn't staying down. At about 40 miles, I stopped and lay down in a roadside stream to make one last attempt to cool off, recover, and go on. After a few minutes, I was able to get up and trudge on, but I still must have looked horrible, because other runners were asking me if I was OK as they passed me.

One of the runners told the crew at the aid station at mile 41 about me and they sent a truck back to see how I was doing. When the driver stopped and asked me if I needed to drop out, I gave it some thought. I didn't *want* to give up. But I was tired, hot, nauseous, in pain, and I still had 60 miles to go and no reason to believe things would get any better. I had already gone through a race's worth of suffering in 2004 just to finish. If I wasn't going to buckle, I wasn't sure I wanted to go through all that again. I got in the truck.

I was quiet during the ride to the aid station, trying to sort out my feelings. In the short term, dropping out relieved all the pressure I was feeling. I might have failed, but I no longer had to deal with the stress of trying to buckle. I could relax for the first time in weeks. Dropping out also ended the worst of the immediate physical suffering.

On the other hand, as the discomfort ebbed, it got harder for me to justify dropping out. I had spent years working towards this day, and I didn't even get halfway to my goal before I gave up. I took pride in my ability to push myself to keep going, and I knew that today I hadn't pushed things to the bitter end. Quitting before I was forced to may have been the wise choice, but I would never know what would have happened if I had stayed in the race. Maybe I could have pulled it together. There were still 60 miles to go, plenty of time to make up what I had lost.

When we got back to the aid station, I had things I needed to do before I could leave the race to lick my wounds, both literal and metaphorical. I found Mark and Karen and told them that we were done for the day. Before we could leave I had to find someone from GAC to pass the message on to Gilly that I wouldn't be there to meet him for the end of the race. While I was looking, I came across Steve Burton and Nancy Given from SRR, who were in Vermont for the USATF Grand Prix race that weekend and had taken a side trip to cheer for me as I went by. I was happy to see them, but embarrassed by the news I had to share. I ended up spending a half-hour wandering around the aid station, talking about why I dropped out, when all I really wanted to do was escape from the scene of my failure.

It was a hard day for everyone. Only about half of the runners at the start made it to the finish, and the winner's time was more than an hour slower than in 2004. None of that made me feel any better about dropping out.

When I ran my first 100 in 2004, I thought I had learned what I needed to know about how hard it was to finish. I thought I was ready to take the next step and run 100 miles as a race. In retrospect, I realized that I had been fortunate in 2004, and that my limited success that year had made me over-confident. Now I'd been reminded yet again that there are always things out of my control that might adversely affect my results in a race. I had to ask myself if I really wanted to spend the time it would require to try again. I had gotten frustrated with running marathons for time, after repeated problems with injuries and weather. Now the same problems were occurring in ultras.

I didn't know if I made another attempt at a 100-mile race with a time goal whether I would deal with the stress any better. The cost in time and effort of preparing for each shot at an ultra was much higher. The rewards for success were greater, but they never seemed to be enough. Every new success left me wanting more. And the risks of failure mounted with every reach for more.

It wasn't like I could just jump into another 100 the next week. There weren't that many to choose from. I would have to wait at least another year to try Vermont again, or I'd have to go to a race that was less convenient and more expensive to get to.

In the meantime, since I had "only" run 40 miles, I was able to spend the rest of my week in Vermont drowning my sorrows in beer, non-competitive running, and general foolishness. The Wednesday after the race, I ran with the hash in Burlington. Then on the weekend I went to a campground in Swanton for the Burlington hash's yearly invitational event. After three days of beer, grilling, running through fields, woods, and leech-infested swamps, pudding wrestling, some naked and semi-naked running, and more beer, I started to put Vermont behind me.

That was the start of a pattern. I would rest, filling up my spare time with drinking, then when I thought I was back on track, I'd build up my training, enter a race, and get injured. I would run through that cycle over and over again, equally dedicated to running and drinking, using beer to wash away my frustration with my running.

In August, while I was still recovering from Vermont, I almost died at a hash in Natick. We had just gotten started and I was searching for the trail when I was stung multiple times by wasps. I ran on, but I began to feel odd and I started to fall behind the pack. My friend Donna looked at me and saw that I had broken out in hives, so she stayed with me. We figured that I was allergic to the stings, which came as a surprise to me since it wasn't the first time I'd been stung.

We slowed to a walk and decided that since we weren't too far from the main road, we should try to get to a drugstore to buy some antihistamine. Before we made it to the road, my vision started to get blurry. A short time later, I fell to the ground. The last thing I remember before I passed out from anaphylactic shock was Donna standing over me, trying to get someone with a cell phone to stop and call 911.

The next thing I knew there were EMTs standing over me. They had just connected a Benedryl IV. That helped me recover enough so they could load me in the ambulance and take me away. I spent an afternoon at the hospital under observation, but I made it back to the hash in time to drink a down-down at the post-run party for "short-cutting trail in an ambulance".

The incident almost got me a new hash name, but everyone was used to "Boner," and "Prophylactic Shock" was hard to say after a few beers.

My back was still bothering me as I tried to get back to regular training. That put a limit on the amount of running I wanted to do. I didn't feel ready to gear up for another ultra. I knew that speedwork was the last thing my back needed, so trying to race against my younger self in shorter races was out. That option didn't really excite me that much anyhow.

I entered a few races, basically living off my previous training for the ultra. That left plenty of time for going out hashing or heading to a bar for a drink with no need to worry about whether it would affect my next run. A few times I had to deal with getting my car fixed after minor incidents on the way home, but I decided not to let that worry me.

In January 2006, it was make-or-break time. My fitness was fading away. Either I was going to start running long again, or I was going to give up. I decided to try a 30-mile run. I managed to run the entire distance, but I probably shouldn't have. Well before I was done, and even with plenty of ibuprofen, my back on fire. After that run, even I realized that I would have to cut back. That left even more time for drinking.

I was also spending time in the dating pool. The women I was dating had a tough time making an impression on me through my drinking, distaste for work, and regret about the limited amount of running I could manage. But I got lucky. In March, I went on my first date with Ruth Sespaniak. Ruth and I had met online, and in one exchange I mentioned that I was going to see "Spamalot," the musical based on the movie comedy "Monty Python and the Holy Grail". Ruth told me she was interested in it. I happened to have an extra ticket, so I asked Ruth if she wanted to go and she said she did.

At the time, I was managing a group that provided computer support within my company. Part of my job was to call people who had given us low ratings on service requests. One of the requests was from a "Ruth Sespaniak," and when I looked up her picture in the company directory, it matched the picture of the person I had met online. So I was very interested to follow up on this particular request, and very relieved to talk to her and find that she seemed like a normal person. At the end of the call, I told her I had one more question for her. I surprised her by asking if she was going to see Spamalot that Friday. She was surprised again to learn that she was going with me!

The day after our first date, I managed to get stopped in Vermont for a DUI (Driving Under the Influence) after a long day of hashing and celebrating St. Patrick's Day. That forced me to slow down for a little while, but soon I was back in the bars and on the trails with the hash.

For some reason Ruth stayed with me, and we were soon seeing each other regularly. Often on days when we didn't have something going on, we'd still see each other at morning in the gym at work. That helped me make it through the long, uninspiring day to follow.

My back pain continued and began to interfere with more than just running. I was having problems sleeping because my back hurt when I lay in certain positions. After visiting a number of different doctors without any success, my insurance company authorized an MRI, which showed some degeneration in a disc in my lower spine. I went to a pain management clinic, where the doctor thought that there might be some extra pressure on some of the spinal nerves near the problem disc. He did a "lumbar facet radiofrequency denervation" to deaden them. Basically, the doctor stuck needles in my spine and ran an RF signal through them to burn out the nerves.

The operation helped reduce the pain, and soon I was able to start building my mileage up again. By April 2007, I had extended my long runs back to more than 20 miles at a time. As always, I wanted to set a goal to test myself against. I still didn't feel 100 percent physically, and even if I did, I wasn't *mentally* ready to go back to ultramarathons. Instead, for lack of anything better to do, I signed up for the Marine Corps Marathon in October. I did some long runs to prepare, but I didn't really take the race seriously. I was now over 45, so my Boston qualifying time had gone up to 3:30. After all the ultras, I was arrogant enough to think that Marine Corps was "only a marathon," and I figured that I could run a 3:30 without too much effort.

Just before the marathon, I got another DUI. This time I totaled my car. Luckily, I wasn't hurt in the accident and I didn't hit anyone else.

It was a turning point. That night was the last time I had anything to drink. I realized that if I kept on the way I was going, I could lose much more than a race. The state forced me to go through an alcohol abuse treatment program, which helped give me a new framework to build on. I keep a picture of my totaled car in my wallet to remind me of what could happen if I slip.

As much as anything else, my relationship with Ruth helped sustain me through the changes I had to make. We were working on something together that meant more than another drink. It's a process that never stops – we're still working on it today.

I was just starting to deal with the fallout from the second DUI when I went to Virginia for the marathon. There were about 30,000 other runners with me at the start, near the Pentagon. It was a beautiful day, not warm or humid as it often is in Northern Virginia, even in October. I was enjoying the surroundings as I ran across the Potomac, through Georgetown, and by all the monuments. At 19 miles I was on track to finish under 3:20. It appeared I would get away with thinking the race was "only a marathon". Then my left calf cramped up. That reduced me to shuffling along at about 11 minutes per mile while hundreds of runners streamed past me. I finally crossed the finish in 3:41.

It took a month for my leg to improve enough to let me run again. I probably should have taken more time, but failing in a marathon had hurt my pride even more. I had quit drinking, but I didn't magically become a different person. My running was still mired in a damaging addictive cycle. I needed to run to feel good about myself.

I was getting more fun from watching Ruth run than I was getting from my own running. She used to run in school, but had let it slide, spending her time hiking, kayaking or cross-country skiing instead. When Ruth started dating me, she realized that if she wanted to spend more time with me, she was going to have to get back into running.

After she started to run, Ruth found she wanted to stick with running for her own sake. She could feel herself getting fitter, losing weight, and learning to run farther and faster. Watching Ruth reap the rewards reminded me of how I felt when I first started running. I was happy I could share that with her.

Ruth decided she wanted to run a half-marathon in February 2008, so I signed up to keep her company. It was only a half-marathon, after all. But I had calf problems again, so I dropped out at about mile 11 and hitchhiked to the finish. I took that as another minor embarrassment. I used to take pride in always finishing races, no matter what. Dropping out in Vermont had been traumatic for me. Sure, it was a 100-mile race, and more than half the people who started that day dropped out, but quitting was something I just didn't do, no matter what. Once that barrier was broken, it didn't seem as important any more for me to limp to the finish if a race wasn't going well. I told myself that it was sometimes best to give up and try again another day, but that still didn't sit well with me emotionally.

After the half-marathon I gave up on racing hard for most of the year. That left me feeling a little empty, but my relationship with Ruth was making up for it. In April we reached the point where we decided to make it permanent, and we got engaged.

I entered some races but treated them more as fun runs or ways to spend time with my friends. I ran a marathon while Ruth and I were in California in May, and later that month I ran Vermont City again to support my friend (and ultra crewperson) Mark while he ran his first one.

One consequence of sobriety was that I didn't have drinking as a crutch to help me make it through another unrewarding day at work. Neither I nor my employers liked the results. My job was hanging by a thread through the summer. It was clear that they were looking to let me go. I finally lost my job early in September 2008. That wasn't a good thing, but it was still something of a relief when it happened.

Soon afterwards, Ruth and I had our wedding. We didn't let my unemployment get in the way of starting off our married life right. Our wedding was outdoors at Kimball Farm in Westford, MA. Along with the ceremony, we had a barbecue, ice cream, and some outdoor fun with our friends and family. One of our friends from SRR, Dan Solomon, got a Justice of the Peace license for the day so he could preside at our wedding. Everyone had a wonderful time. There was a lot of rain on our wedding day, but that just added a little extra water to the splashing from the bumper boats.

The next day our wedding party joined Ruth and me in a 5K. We ran wearing t-shirts labeling us as the "bride" and "groom". Then we packed our running shoes and kayaks and headed off to Cape Cod for our honeymoon.

Through all this I was building my weekly mileage back up again. It was a Sisyphean task, but it's what I do. Now that I had lost my job, I had even more time for running. By the end of 2008, I was regularly hitting 40 miles per week and had a couple of weeks where I reached 60 miles, something I'd never done before unless 30 or more of the miles were coming from a single long run.

That got me to thinking about goals again. Running within my limits wasn't enough for me. I still needed to push against those limits and get my racing fix. I told myself that training for a fast marathon wouldn't be too much for me to handle. I was putting in plenty of miles, so I figured all I needed to do was add a little speedwork and I'd be set to go.

I decided that my first step would be to start going to SRR indoor track workouts. I avoided them in the past because I always seemed to break down when I ran track, but I knew that if I wanted to run a fast marathon, I needed to find a way to add some speed to my running. Ruth was going to track, and it seemed like a good way to spend more time with her and my SRR friends.

I started track early in December. By the end of December I was having intermittent sharp pains in my back. By the middle of January, my left calf hurt again. I declared the experiment with track over, only a month-and-a-half after it started.

Ruth was still growing steadily as a runner. She was ready to try a longer race, so in March 2009, we entered the Eastern

States 20 Miler. Race day was miserable. The temperatures were just barely above freezing, and we ran the whole race in a cold rain. There were 20 mph winds coming from the North. Luckily, they were tailwinds for most of the race, so we didn't feel their full effect until we were standing outside after the race in our heavy, wet gear.

I ran easily, well under a 7:30 pace, for about 12 miles. Then I started to slow down. I figured I was just out of racing condition, but it was more than that. By the last couple of miles, I was struggling to drag myself along at less than 9 minutes per mile. I managed to hold on and finish just under 2:30, but after the race I had some back pain and my hamstrings felt tighter than usual.

The back pain ebbed after some rest, but my legs never regained their spring. I developed a case of "runner's butt," a persistent pain where my left hamstrings attached to my hip. When my hamstrings tightened with each step forward, they tugged painfully on the area that hurt. I was reduced to a gait where all I could do was use my left quadriceps to flip my leg ahead of me so I could slowly limp along.

Finally, even I understood that I had to shut things down. I cut my mileage way back in April and started going to physical therapy for the pain. It took until October before I could get back to running 20 miles per week on a semi-regular basis. The runner's butt didn't disappear, but it receded enough to let me run, and I learned how to manage the residual pain to keep it from increasing while I started building up my mileage yet again.

I lost a lot of my fitness while I was going through therapy. Those six months were the longest break I'd taken from running since I began in 1992. It had been a long time since 10 miles was a long and hard run for me. Ramping my mileage up again was almost like going back to my time as a novice distance runner. I found it interesting, if not always fun, to have to push myself to extend my long run to 12 or 15 miles. I'd forgotten how a Saturday morning 15-mile run could be difficult, and how even that distance could leave me drained and wanting a nap afterwards.

But I persevered, and by February 2010 my weekly mileage was back into the 30s and my long run was up to 18 miles. Ruth was needed to fill out the SRR women's master's team at a hilly USATF-Grand Prix 10-mile race in Amherst, so off we went. The result? My left calf went out again. The rock rolled back to the bottom of the hill.

Ruth also had a sore hamstring after Eastern States. She took a break, got it taken care of, and when she felt completely better, started running again. In 2010, while I was struggling, she was training for her first marathon, injury-free. Maybe stubborn denial isn't the way to go after all.

The first exchange zone at the 2009 Lake Winnipesaukee
Relay

Chapter 11: Why keep running?

"Why do I keep running? That's more complicated. The fitness is still part of it, but it's also for that running feeling. "What?!?," you say. It's when I'm out running on a road and there are no cars, no dogs, the wind is in my face, and the sun is shining, or maybe it's not. It's the sound of my own breathing, which is like a mantra in a bizarre way. I run for that feeling when my legs just go, and all is right in my world. Oh yeah, and so I can eat."
- Karen Bates

Addiction is often called "the disease of more". When you're addicted to something, you can never get enough of it. The amount that used to be sufficient to satisfy you isn't adequate anymore.

Another sign that you're addicted is when your relationship with whatever you're addicted to causes problems and you continue the relationship in spite of those problems.

By those criteria, I am clearly addicted to running.

But running isn't really bad for me, right? I've had a lot of fun running and I want to keep doing it. I enjoy the company of my running friends when we're racing, out on long runs, or eating pizza at Casey's. The exercise and fresh air are good for me. If I don't run, I'll end up fat, sitting on the couch with my TV remote and my bag of chips, waiting to die of a heart attack. I need to run!

I had a lot of fun while I was drinking. I still miss relaxing and enjoying the company of my friends with a drink or two, or winding down in a bar with a beer after a run or some other event. And a drink or two every day is good for my heart! I even miss a lot of the outrageously dumb (but funny) stuff I've done when I didn't stop after a drink or two.

My relationship with alcohol changed over time until my search for more fun actually resulted in less fun. When I finally realized that my drinking was causing problems that were outweighing the fun I tried to drink moderately. Unfortunately, after the first drink or two moderation usually seemed like a good idea for some other day. Finally, I realized that the only way to avoid the problems created by my alcohol use was to put drinking aside. Some people can drink responsibly, but I've gotten into enough trouble to know the risks aren't worth it.

Most addiction treatment programs agree. They believe that abstinence is the only way to manage an addiction and avoid the problems that it causes. They think that anyone who believes they can learn to moderate their behavior and have a healthy relationship instead of an addictive relationship is in denial, not in touch with their true situation.

If that's true about a running addiction, then I choose to stay in denial. I want to keep chasing the runner's high. I'm still going to run.

Not every runner is an addict. The runners I have met over the years can be divided into four different groups.

The first group is the new runners. New runners are still trying to figure it out. Running is hard for them. They may have worked their way up to running 3 or 4 miles at a time, but each run is a grind. They often have doubts about whether they're going to keep running, and some of them don't. But if they stick with it, they start to notice changes. They lose weight, their muscle tone improves, running gets easier, and they might even start to toy with the idea of running further or entering a race.

The next group of runners is the fitness runners. Fitness runners have stuck with running long enough to understand the benefits. They enjoy how running helps them stay healthy and build strength and stamina that they can use in their other activities. Fitness runners have made running a part of their life. Their bodies are accustomed to running and no longer change as fast as a new runner's. Further improvement is still possible, but it requires more work than before. However, fitness runners don't worry much about becoming a better runner. A fitness runner may enter a few races, mostly local 5 or 10Ks, but they're casual about it. If they're traveling or on vacation and it's inconvenient to run, they have no problem taking a week or two off. They have few injuries. When they are injured, they back off and take the time to get better before they resume their usual running routine.

The third group is the racers. Most running addicts are in this group.

Someone becomes a racer when they start to set competitive goals for their running. Racers' goals may involve successfully competing against other people in races, or successfully competing against themselves by improving their time at a particular distance. It isn't always about speed. Sometimes their competitive efforts are about pushing themselves to add another marathon, another consecutive day of running, or another week with a high mileage total in their running log. Whatever the goal, for racers running is about keeping score.

Racers plan their running, and often their life outside of running, so everything contributes towards reaching their goals. They judge every run as a success or failure by whether the run helped them advance towards their current goal.

There's nothing more rewarding to a racer than reaching a goal. But a win or a PR only provides momentary satisfaction, and then it's time to move on, time to set a new goal and try to do even better. The past is past. The future is an opportunity to do more.

For some racers, accomplishing their running goals can get to be an obsession. Unfortunately, always striving to go farther or faster causes problems. The physical and mental stress racers create by always pushing themselves for more makes them more susceptible to injury. Racers often deny their injuries as long as they can in order to keep running. Their injuries get worse until they finally force the racers to stop. Ironically, since they delayed treatment in order to keep running, they often end up staying out longer because of the severity of their ailments. Each additional day without running is torture for the racers. They feel their fitness ebbing, their weight piling on, and their goals slipping away.

For a few people, those who are competing for something concrete, like a scholarship, prize money, or Olympic medals, taking the racer lifestyle to the extreme might make sense. Other people, who dedicate their lives to racing out of personal pride, are often trying to fill some less practical need for success or approval or belonging in order to build their self-esteem. Unfortunately, no matter how fast they are, there's always someone faster. Comparing yourself to others is never the most realistic way to become happy with who you are.

It doesn't have to be a bad thing to be a racer. The goals of a racer are clearer and success is easier to measure and more under the control of the individual compared to other tasks in life, like working with a difficult boss, writing a book, or raising a child. If your body can handle the strain and you can manage your efforts without becoming obsessive, a life focused on running can be as fulfilling as any other kind of life.

The fourth and final group is the mature runners. They have gone through the racer phase, so they know what it's like to take things all the way to the edge, and sometimes beyond. But the mature runners have learned to compromise. They don't let running control their life.

A mature runner is a lot like a fitness runner, in that they run at a level that allows them to reap the health benefits without the downside of excessive racing. But mature runners value the act of running for many reasons, not just for what running does for their physical well-being.

Mature runners still have goals, but they don't need their goals to create meaning for their running. They aren't driven to reach their goals at all costs. The goals of a mature runner aren't barriers to break through, they're just mile markers on their course through life.

Mature runners know where their limits are, and they know that exceeding those limits will cause problems, so they don't try. That reduces the number and severity of the injuries mature runners get, and since they take the time to let their aches and pains heal, the few injuries that do occur don't linger. They get to spend as much time running as they want, because they aren't greedy. They have found the balance between their desire to run and the demands of the other parts of their lives.

For a long time, I've been a racer. That's caused problems for me. The chief motivator for my daily runs has been to get ready for my next target race. I like to think I may finally be ready to change my primary goals from the timebound and concrete to something more nebulous, something I can always work on, but never need to finish.

I'm not quite there yet. For example, I've been wearing my shirt from the 2005 Vermont 100 as a reminder that I failed to break 24 hours and a goad to keep working on that piece of unfinished business. A mature runner would wear his 2004 Vermont 100 t-shirt to celebrate a day of success or, more likely, he would wear the shirt from an obscure 5K because it's comfortable and it's dyed a pleasant blue color.

I still have plenty of concrete goals. My main goal is to keep running into my seventies and eighties. If I can keep going that long, not only will I have years of running enjoyment ahead of me, but when I reach that age I'll be sure to be winning races by sheer attrition. If I'm bringing home age group trophies by virtue of being the only one at that age left running, that's fine by me.

Every runner, no matter how fast they are and how hard they work, eventually gets to the point where they quit improving. New PRs stop happening, and soon they can't even keep up with what they used to be able to do. Their race times increase, as does their need for recovery time. They can no longer compete with the runner they used to be, let alone all those fast younger people.

A study of 2004 New York Marathon finishers found that starting at age 19 and continuing until age 27, the average runner got faster every year. Then performance declined as the runners got older. The good news is that the decline rate was slower. The results for older runners were faster than the teenagers' times until age 64.

For individuals, there is a rule of thumb that says most people who train regularly can continue to improve for about 10 years before they reach their peak. So, if you don't start running regularly until age 45 you may be able to keep improving until you get to be 55 or so. I started running regularly when I was 31. My time for getting faster is over.

I need to accept that I'll never accomplish some of the speed goals that I've had for a long time. I haven't run a sub-40 10K, a sub-1:30 half marathon, a marathon under the 3:10 open qualifying time for Boston (let alone a sub-3), or a sub-24 hour 100-mile race.

As a racer, I hate to admit failure. I'm also a firm believer that if I haven't given up on trying to reach a goal, I haven't failed. But if I'm going to become a mature runner, I have to let go of those speed goals and change my attitude about falling short. Giving up on an impractical goal is only a failure if I call it that. The mind frame that sees it as failure is never satisfied. Even if I did realize a particular goal, there would always be another, faster time that I didn't reach.

Striving for speed is what causes most of my problems. I still fall into the trap of thinking that if I put the right plan together and put in enough effort, I can run as fast as or faster now than I ever could. I know that there was room for improvement when I was younger, so I figure all I have to do is train a little more carefully and I can work hard enough to get faster without getting hurt.

Then I get to race day, and when it's time to make a choice I sacrifice my long-term goal of enduring running continuity for better results in today's race. Of course, in the end that means I don't get either one.

I've consistently shown that my heart and lungs are fit enough to support my mind's desire to run long distances at a faster pace than my muscles and joints can tolerate. It's hard to rein myself in just to avoid getting hurt. It feels like I'm slacking off, doing less than I'm capable of. So I don't hold back until it's too late and a new pain forces me to pull up.

One of the seductive qualities of racing is the illusion of control. In running it's easy to see the clock as the objective measure of success or failure. In other areas of life it can be hard for me to figure out how to succeed or even to define success. I often need the help and approval of other people to accomplish something, and I get frustrated when I don't get what I think I need. When I started running it seemed like success was up to me. I found that if I put in more miles and ran harder than usual from time to time, I would get faster. I was captivated, addicted to that feeling of control.

Alcoholics Anonymous says that if an addict wants to quit drinking, first he has to admit he can't control his alcohol consumption. To become a mature runner, I have to let go of the idea that I'm in complete control of my running. Perfection, however you define it, cannot be achieved by man or woman. The pursuit of perfection, while accepting we'll never get there, is the best we can do. It's an ongoing battle to accept that, but if I learn to do it for my running, that'll help me with other aspects of my life.

In the end, successful racing is about winning. Luckily, running isn't just about racing. I'm reasonably fast for a human, though not as fast as I once was. It was evident early on that there would always be someone faster in almost every race. I've learned to lose to other people with only minor amounts of jealousy – I've certainly had enough practice. I need to learn to lose to my younger self with similar grace.

Many people continue to compete when they get older by trying different challenges, like age group racing or triathlons. I started running ultramarathons in my 40's, and I'm looking forward to turning 50 and racing in a new age group. But no matter what I do, if I measure success with a clock I'll reach a point of diminishing returns.

I'm hoping I'll learn to accept my limitations on the road to becoming a mature runner, but I still have learning to do. When Ruth ran the 2010 Sugarloaf Marathon, it was her first marathon. I wanted the day to be about her, so I didn't register to run. I even skipped the 15K held at the same time. Besides, I hadn't run farther than 18 miles in more than a year because of injuries. Also, I had been sick with a stomach flu the week before the race, so I was still shaky from three days of 100-plus fever and I hadn't eaten properly for a week. Running a marathon was not a prudent idea.

The race was on Sunday. We were going to drive back

right after the race, leaving no time for me to run, so I went for a short run Saturday morning and then we left for Maine, leaving my running gear at home.

At our hotel, we checked the weather. The forecast called for a gorgeous day for running, sunny, in the 50s, and with a 15 mph tailwind on most of the point-to-point course. We headed out to pick up Ruth's number and drive the course. It was a lovely route, passing by beautiful rivers, forests, and mountains. By the time we'd driven halfway through the course all my good intentions were forgotten, and I was trying to figure out how I could run. If it hadn't been a two-hour drive to the nearest place where I could buy running shoes, I probably would have registered.

It's not easy trying to be responsible. Even after a couple of years of sobriety I often find I still have to resist the urge to drink. It has gotten easier over time to deal with the urge, but it's still there. I suspect the urge to push myself to extend my limits when I'm running will be just as hard to break. The simple clarity of time can make it hard to remember that there are other types of success.

I still use goals for motivation, but those goals have to change as I start to slow down.

Some people start accumulating runs or races. They're still measuring success by numbers, but now they're trying for larger numbers to demonstrate their sheer persistence instead of smaller numbers (times or finishing positions) to show their speed. These people might start trying to build a long streak of consecutive days of running. Or they might try to complete marathons in all 50 states or on all seven continents.

Those particular goals don't work for me. I'd rather target scenic or fun places to run or visit, instead of going somewhere less interesting just to check off one more box on an arbitrary list. If you want to choose a marathon because it allows you to check off both one state out of fifty and one month out of 12 (or one week out of 52, as some people have done lately), that's your choice. I'm happy with the local 5K near my vacation spot, especially if it has a barbecue afterwards.

I do have a few goals that involve accumulating runs. I run in the Mill Cities and Lake Winnipesaukee relays every year with teams from SRR. I've run four of the five Mill Cities legs and seven out of eight legs at Lake Winnie. This year, I plan to complete both sets of relay legs.

I've never earned the IronRunner jacket for running the entire USATF-NE Grand Prix series in a single year. There's always been a conflict with another race or an injury that has kept me out of at least one event. This year, both problems occurred. Maybe 2012 will be the year. I'll be over 50 for all the races that year, and I might be able to score for the team in my new age group.

I'm not sure if there are more ultramarathons in my future. I'd like to have the fitness to run ultras again, and I like the idea of being someone who runs ultramarathons without a time goal. Running a trail ultra usually means meeting a friendly, relaxed group of people and sharing a long trip through some beautiful countryside. Ultras on asphalt and concrete are much harder on my body, but there are a few that I'd like to try someday, like the SRR 24 Hour Around the Lake or the Comrades Marathon in South Africa.

One of the things I like most about running is how I sometimes drift into a zone where I have no worries about what happened in the past and no anxiety about what might happen in the future. Consistent effort towards a clear goal and the metronomic beat of my footsteps combine to focus my attention on what I'm doing at the moment. Nothing but running gets me into that zen-like state of calm effort. An ultra's worth of that is something incredibly valuable to me.

I don't know if I could stay healthy enough if I tried to put in the miles I'd need to train for ultras. And I'm not sure I can (or really want to) put in the time to train and still keep a healthy balance with my relationships and other activities. But there's no hurry to decide. Ultras are an older runner's sport.

I have managed to attain some of the qualities of a mature runner. I do a lot more running now just for enjoyment, without a particular goal race in mind. I've always been something of a mileage junkie. I like watching my weekly mileage totals accumulate in my log. I'd like to settle in and regularly run 35 or 40 miles a week, with a long run of about 20 miles every couple of weeks. One of the most important things I've learned from all my years of running is that the only way to make a 5-mile run fun is to run 10 miles. A 20-mile run is long enough to give me plenty of shorter options I can run comfortably that are still long enough to keep me interested.

On long runs I enjoy the company of my friends who are training for a marathon or some other race. Some of them find it odd that I'll do a 20-mile run just for fun. It's in how you look at it. My body may not be fit enough to run 50 or 100 miles, but my brain still is. Ultramarathoning trained my brain to see a 20-mile run as hard, but not *that* hard.

Since I met Ruth I've had a lot of fun reliving some of my past, watching her find out how rewarding it is to put the effort in to training and get concrete results. And running is a great way for us to spend time outdoors, talking or just being together.

Ruth has helped remind me yet again that even though I've gone out for a run thousands of times, new things are always mixing in with the routine. There's always somewhere new to run or someone new to run with.

And new experiences continue to find me. Small changes can keep me amused. I've never had much in the way of facial hair, but last fall I let my beard and mustache grow for an improv comedy show I was performing in. When winter came, finishing a run with sweat frozen in my beard was something new for me.

Other times, unknown forces pull together to create something unique, just for me. I was out on a beautiful sunny day on one of my innumerable runs alongside the Mystic Lakes when I saw a leaf outlined against the blue sky, floating in midair. I stopped, expecting to watch it fall, but the leaf continued to defy gravity. It was a magical illusion, one that wasn't spoiled by finding there was an invisible thread of spider silk holding the leaf in place.

In March 2008, I was entering my mileage for the weekend into my running log when I noticed that my "total lifetime mileage" since I started keeping a log in 1992 had reached 19,999 miles. Twenty thousand miles isn't an enormous number compared to what some of my friends have done in the same period. Still, running 20,000 miles in less than 16 years does indicate a certain amount of consistency and persistence. I take pride in that, and every day I continue to run reinforces that feeling.

My first podiatrist said I probably shouldn't try to run a marathon. Eighteen marathons (and a few longer races) later, it's safe to say I've exceeded his expectations. I've done a lot of that through desire and sheer stubbornness. When I think back on how painful some of those miles were and how many times I've had to pick things up again after an injury, maybe I could have tried restraint a little more often.

Now my times aren't what they used to be. I'll always have a certain wistful longing for when I could run faster or go on seemingly forever. But as long as I just keep running, I can find satisfaction in that simple fact.

All that running has taken a lot of time. As some point I

have to ask if it's been worth it. It can be pretty selfish, setting aside an hour or more for myself almost every day to get ready to run, run, and clean up afterwards. And I've had issues that may not have been directly related to running, but were entwined with my running life. For a while, between weekly bar runs, hashing, and post-pub race parties, it was getting hard to tell whether I was running so I could drink, or drinking so I could run.

It is worth it. Life is often about difficult things I have to do. Running is a (sometimes) difficult thing I choose to do. Running has helped me prove to myself that I can persevere and accomplish something hard, through good times, but also through bad weather, injuries, and those days where doing anything seems like an effort. That has helped me get through other challenges in life, like quitting drinking. Running helps with more mundane issues too. There are many tedious and repetitive, but necessary, tasks that I don't like to deal with, things like cleaning house, mowing the lawn, or going to work every day. Learning to run marathons doesn't make sitting through yet another pointless meeting at work into something fun, but it has taught me that I can survive an hour or two of pain (physical or mental) and come back for more the next day.

Running regularly creates a foundation that supports me. I'm always trying to pace myself and run strongly and smoothly for my entire run. The regular beat of a solid, steady pace helps me live in the moment and calmly contemplate the trials that I'll face over the next few miles and the ones that I'll have to contend with after I've put my running shoes away for the day.

Sometimes, when I least expect it, there's joy. My body glides down the road effortlessly with my mind riding atop in harmony. The synchronicity between body and mind is so strong that my body starts to flow along a little faster before any whim for speed surfaces into my conscious thoughts. The magic can happen in little spurts during any run. Longer runs create room for those spurts to stretch out. Sometimes the feeling extends to the whole run.

But I can't make that happen. I never find that fluidity on days when I strive too hard, which is why I seldom find it on race day. The few times that I've felt the flow during a race were some of my fastest races. The only time I went under 19 minutes in a 5K, it felt so easy I thought the course must have been short. I don't feel the magic when I'm consciously backing off on my level of effort either. I have to earn it, but I can't be greedy. But sometimes, when I'm relaxed and appreciative of the simple pleasures of running, I get a little glimpse of transcendence.

The rest of the time I settle, and it's still good. Each run is worthy in its own way, even when it's only for the relief I feel when a bad run is over. And every run helps keep me fit so I'm ready the next time the magic appears.

That's the difference between running and chemically induced euphoria. One you can buy, the other you have to earn. You can give up, go passive, and still drink and smoke and snort to get high. But if you want the runner's high, you have to find a way to carry on.

I'm going to keep running. Sometimes I stumble across a moment of fulfillment, sometimes I get lost on the road, but if I keep putting one foot in front of the other eventually I know I'll find the path that takes me home.

Running in the fog during the
2009 July 4th Around Mount Desert Island Relay

Appendix 1 - Advice for the New Runner

"I have been running for almost 2 years, which I know still counts me as a newbie in most people's eyes. Then again I don't see myself ever stopping, which means that someday, I too can be like the 64-year old gentleman I met in a race yesterday who has run 21 marathons and 8 Bostons."
- Jane Parkin Kullmann

Since this is a book about running, I need to have a chapter about training. I think there might be a law that requires it.

It's easy to start running. All you need is a pair of shoes and a pair of shorts. Some people choose to get by without the shoes, and fearlessly stride barefoot through the debris of modern life.

For most people, starting to run is not quite that simple. If nothing else, most people live in places where variations in weather conditions mean they'll need more than just shoes and shorts. But gear aside, many people who are just starting to run have no idea how to proceed, nor any confidence that what they're going to do is what's best for them.

There's no need to worry. The most difficult step is making the commitment to start running regularly. After that, there are many ways to proceed, perhaps as many as there are runners. It helps to have a plan, but when you're starting out your plan doesn't have to be too detailed. As long as you don't try to do too much too fast, you'll be fine. You can always make changes to your plan as you improve. You'll soon find you're capable of feats that will surprise you.

Every guide for beginning runners starts with a warning. They always recommend that you visit your doctor before you start an exercise program to ensure that it's safe for you to begin. My view is that for most people, the best thing for you to do is start that exercise program. Just be sure to start at a level of effort that's not out of your reach, and ramp the effort up slowly. Better too slow than too fast. Walking is a great way to start – it's just a slow form of running.

Of course, if you have a heart problem, asthma, or some other medical issue, visit your doctor for specific advice for your situation. If your doctor advises you not to run, even if you're going to start slowly and easily, my advice to you is to find another doctor.

You will need shoes and clothes to get started. There's no need to go overboard at first. The shorts and t-shirts you already have are probably good enough for a while. As you spend more time running, you'll want to look into clothing that is more comfortable. But if you prefer to go shopping for color-coordinated, sweat-wicking outfits right away, go ahead. Whatever makes you feel better about running is a good thing. A big part of getting into a regular routine of running is mental. If dressing in special running clothes helps you keep to your routine, or if the guilt of wasting money by not using the running clothes you bought gets you out the door, do whatever works!

When you're starting out the most critical equipment to buy is a good pair of running shoes. You can run in anything, even dress shoes, but most runners do best in shoes designed for running. There's a bewildering array of choices available, but choosing a shoe doesn't have to be that complicated.

For your first pair of shoes, look for a basic model without any special gimmicks, what the manufacturers call a "neutral" shoe. When you get into shape and start running more, you might find that you need additional support or more cushioning, but until you've done some running and learn what you need, something simple is usually best.

You've probably been walking and running in neutral

shoes your whole life, so you're used to them. A shoe with a lot of extra cushioning may feel great in the store, but it may not be stable enough for you. A motion control shoe may be too stable and force your body into unnatural movement patterns. Both can cause problems instead of fixing them.

A basic, neutral shoe is the conservative way to get started. Also, a simple shoe will usually be cheaper. Avoid the expensive top-of-the-line shoe with all the gadgetry. Even if you do need some form of assistance, you can usually find another option that accomplishes the same goal at a lower price.

The fit is more important than any gimmicks. If your shoe doesn't fit properly you'll get blisters and other annoying aches and pains when you run. Your shoes need to have plenty of room for your toes so your toenails don't rub against the shoe. If there's not enough room, your toenails will take a beating and they'll turn black and fall off. Your shoes also need to be the proper width. Make sure they're not too tight, as your feet will expand a little when you run.

Be practical, not vain. Pretty colors are nice, but function is more important than appearance. It might be important to you to wear a size five dress shoe, but if the running shoe that fits right is a seven, buy the seven. I was in a running store one day when a woman who was trying on a pair of clunky-looking training shoes asked me if they made her look fat. That's not what she should worry about. If she buys the right shoe and uses it to run regularly, her butt will shrink. The benefits from the right shoes will outweigh (ha!) any issues with the way they look on her feet.

Running shoe salespeople can be very helpful in picking a shoe. But don't let them talk you into something that doesn't seem right. You're the only one that really knows how the shoe feels at the end of your leg.

When you try on shoes keep in mind that running shoes always seem more comfortable in the store than they will after you've run in them for a while. A new pair of shoes comes with a soft insole that feels great at first but compresses to almost nothing after a run or two.

A good store will let you try shoes on a treadmill or take them for a short outdoor run if it's dry outside. Unfortunately, no short test can substitute for an extended test under real running conditions. No matter how careful you are, you're likely to make a mistake and buy shoes that aren't right for you. The best stores will let you return those problem shoes, for store credit at least, once you find they don't work for you in the real world.

Good socks will help protect you from any rough spots in your shoes. While there are almost as many different socks as there are shoes, a basic pair of athletic socks will get you started. Just make sure there are no seams rubbing against your feet. Sometimes it helps to turn the socks inside out so the seams are on the outside. If you do get blisters when you start running, you might want to try socks designed for running before you worry about trying another pair of relatively expensive shoes. Running socks have fewer seams and are made of materials that wick sweat away.

Once you've dressed, it's time to start running. There are a ton of training plans for the beginning runner out there. You can easily find a perfectly good plan in books, magazines, or on the Internet. Or you can just create your own, keeping safe and increasing your chance of success by following a few simple guidelines.

The most important rule to keep in mind when you're beginning to run is "Start slowly, then ease off." If you overdo it when you're starting out as a runner you're more likely to suffer unpleasantly or maybe even hurt yourself. Oddly enough, most people don't really enjoy suffering.

If you're in good shape from some other activity like biking or swimming, you need to be especially careful not to run as hard as you can right away. Running will use your muscles and tendons differently, so if you're not careful your biking fitness just gives you the ability to really hurt yourself by running too hard too soon.

Your goal as a new runner is to establish a regular routine. That's hard enough for most people. Add in a discouraging amount of discomfort and that makes it more likely that someday you'll decide to miss a day for extra rest "just this once". Once you start finding reasons to skip your run it's a short step to quitting. It's better to make it easy on yourself while you develop your running habit. There'll be plenty of time later to push yourself harder.

It's always a good idea to have your running schedule planned out ahead of time. There's always a good reason to skip your run if you're looking for one. It's easier to make the decision when to run ahead of time, when you're sitting comfortably and the actual run is safely off in the future. Then when the time to run arrives, you skip the part where you decide whether or not you want to run. Tell yourself the decision has already been made. Don't think, just go.

Most people don't actually run every day, nor at the same time every day. Work or family obligations can get in the way. Maybe you usually run in the morning, but you want to meet up with other people once a week for an evening run. Take all that into consideration when you set up your plan. Three or four days a week is plenty, especially when you're starting out.

Setting goals can help motivate you to run regularly, but keep the goals simple. When you're starting an exercise program for the first time you'll do best if your goal is simply to set a routine and stick to it. If you go running when it's time to run, whether or not it's "too hot" or "too cold" or there's something good on television, that's something you can be proud of. Keeping to your routine in spite of distractions will be hard enough for now. Soon enough it'll be time to worry about how far or how fast you can go. Don't worry about running a marathon just yet.

Continue to keep it simple when you're choosing *where* you're going to run. I find it easiest to use a route that starts and ends at my own front door. That way I spend my time running, not traveling to where I'm going to run. If you live in a city where the streets are crowded with cars and the sidewalks crowded with people, or in a suburb where the traffic is fast and the sidewalks are few, do what you have to do to find a place where you're comfortable. But if you don't need to get in the car and drive to a track or a park to run, you'll have fewer excuses to skip a day. You'll also get to know your neighborhood better if you travel it on foot instead of in a car. Later, when you're in better shape and have more options, you can look for other places to run.

If you're starting from the couch, I suggest that you pick a single route and stick with it a while instead of changing the route from day to day. The more choices you need to make before you run, the more likely you are to choose not to run. More importantly, it will be easy for you to see how much you're improving when you run the same route every day. That will help motivate you to keep going.

I always like to run on a loop course instead of going out and back on the same route. Out and back courses are good if you live in an isolated area and all the loop courses are too long for you while you're getting started, or if you're traveling and want to keep from getting lost. If you can, you probably want to avoid any major hills for now.

Three miles is a good distance to start with. A 3-mile

loop, even if you start by walking the whole way, takes less than an hour to complete. A lot of the health benefits of running come from extending your workout to where you're elevating your heart rate for 30 or 40 minutes at a time. Even if you're walking instead of running, you're better off than you would be if you started with a shorter distance.

Once you pick your course, begin by alternating running for a minute with walking for a minute until you make it all the way around the entire loop. If that's too hard, start by walking the whole way. As you get in better shape, start making the running intervals between your one-minute walking breaks longer. Run for two, then three, then four minutes at a time before slowing to a walk. You might want to buy a runner's watch with a repeating timer to help measure the intervals. Once you've worked your way up to where the running segments are somewhere around eight minutes long, try running the whole distance.

Try to extend the amount you run at regular intervals. Give yourself a week or two to get used to your current level of effort, and then increase the duration of your running interval. But if you have a bad day or need a little more time to get ready for the next level don't force yourself into doing that day's entire workout. Improvement isn't always consistent. If you feel like a run isn't going as well as you'd like, dial it back that day, take more walks, and try to get back on track next time.

I'll say it again – Be patient. Run EASILY when you start out! Soon enough you'll notice that your runs are getting faster, even though you're not working any harder. Never hurry; there'll be plenty of time to worry about how fast you're going later.

Don't even time your workouts. If you're at all competitive, timing your runs will encourage you to try and go faster each time you go out. That will only push you to try and do too much. When you're a new runner you should be more concerned with running farther, not faster.

Build your own plan from these suggestions or use a plan you find online, read in a magazine, or get from a friend. If the first plan you try doesn't work for you, don't worry and definitely don't give up. Just try something else until you find a routine that fits the way you live. Remember: everyone is different. Don't strain trying to keep to a particular schedule or keep up with other people out of pride or to prove a point.

Once you've gotten far enough away from your former couch-potato status there comes a time where you need to decide whether you're going to keep up with your new-found running habit. It takes most people a little time to learn whether they're destined to become a runner. It's important to stick it out long enough to build enough fitness so you aren't pushing your limits every time you run. It may be hard to imagine, but I promise that if you stick with your routine long enough you'll get over a hump and there will be days where running is almost effortless.

Hang in there until you're fit enough to regularly run 3 miles or more. That's probably enough to know how much you'll really like running. People who quit before they put in the time and build up their endurance to a reasonable level are just wasting their effort.

If you've built some endurance and have the ability to run a few miles without exhausting yourself but you're still asking yourself whether or not to go every time you have a run planned, running may not be right for you. A few people enjoy the side benefits of losing weight or being in better shape for other activities enough to grit their teeth and grind through their runs. But most people, if they don't really like running for its own sake, find it tough to stick it out.

Ask yourself, "Is this fun? Is this what I want to be doing with my time?" If you're thinking about quitting any time you get a little tired or slightly bored, maybe you should look for another activity. That's nothing to be ashamed about.

On the other hand, when you get to where you're running 3 miles regularly, that's not only a good start towards incorporating running into a healthier lifestyle, but maybe – just maybe - you might want to think about running in a local 5 kilometer (3.1 mile) race. Be careful – you might get addicted.

Finishing leg 1 at Lake Winnipesaukee in 2007

Appendix 2 - Even More Advice

"You'll laugh at this, but the downfall of being a forefoot striker is that I never look awesome in pictures, unless I'm in an all-out sprint. My legs are always underneath me, so I look slow. It's kind of depressing when I look at pictures of myself and my much slower friends, but they look fast and badass, and I look like I'm jogging."
-Rachael Shanley

Running doesn't have to be all about training to get faster or run farther. Once you reach a level of ability you're happy with it's perfectly reasonable to settle into a routine where you enjoy running for fitness and as part of a comfortable, active lifestyle. Even if you do go to races, you don't have to train for them. There's no reason you can't enjoy getting together with new and old friends and running as well as you can that day, without worrying about whether you could go faster if you "trained".

I, on the other hand, have often wanted to see how fast and how far I can run, and then I wanted to see if I could go faster and farther than that. I also want to see if I can beat my running buddy or that guy I see every morning running the other way in his Boston Marathon jacket. Running haphazardly won't get me there. When I want to step up my running program, I need to follow some kind of training plan.

If you want to train as hard as you can tolerate in order to see how fast you can run, more power to you. It's a risky choice. The more you push yourself, the more likely you are to have a problem. To maximize your potential, you have to work right along the edge of what you can tolerate, and sometimes you're going to go over that edge.

These days I skip track workouts and most other forms of high-speed training. Those high-intensity workouts are more likely to cause injuries and I've always been injury-prone. Sadly, healing takes longer with each passing year so the increased risk of injury just isn't worth it.

Everybody has to make choices. If you want to be the best runner you can be, you have to choose to take risks and skip other opportunities. You have to spend time on running that you could have spent with your family, on biking or other sports, or on writing, singing, painting, carpentry, or whatever other activities interest you. On the other hand, if you want to be the best father, biker, writer, etc..., that has to cut into your running time. There's no reason you can't be good at multiple things, but if you want to be the best at any single thing, you have to focus on it and leave the others for cross-training or relaxing.

I'm not going to give you any specific training plans. There are plenty of examples of detailed plans available online, in other books, in magazines, or from other runners, or maybe you belong to a running club with a coach who can help you get started. Whatever you start with, don't take it as gospel. Feel free to make changes based on what you learn about how you react to the program. One size does not fit all. Build your personal training plan based on what it is *you* are trying to accomplish. Then, as you progress keep the following guidelines in mind.

Endurance is the base upon which everything else is built. You can't worry about how fast you can run 5 miles until you have the endurance to run 5 miles. Then, the best way to make that 5-mile run easy is to develop the endurance to run 10 miles. If you run 20 miles a week, you'll probably improve more by moving up to 30 miles a week than you will by making some kind of speed workout part your 20-mile week.

Once you've built a reasonable base the concept of "specificity" comes into play. It's a simple idea. To reach your maximum potential, you need to make some choices.

If you're training for a short, fast race, more of your training should consist of shorter, faster running. If you're training for a longer run, you want to spend more time doing long runs. If you're training for ultramarathons, you might not do any speed work at all. If you want to do everything -- if you want to run 5Ks, marathons, and maybe even longer races -- you probably won't be as good at any one of them as you could be.

Once you start doing specific hard workouts, whether they're speedwork or long runs, it's important to realize that improvement doesn't happen just from doing hard workouts. You need to work hard, but you also need to allow yourself time to recover from working hard. A hard workout (or a race) tears your body down. If you don't allow your body enough time to recover after a big effort, you just keep tearing it down further. Then, instead of improving you get slower. You may find that you lack the energy to get out and run. You're more prone to injury or sickness. Life sucks.

On the other hand, if you allow enough time for recovery after each hard workout, you end up fitter than you were before. People who study athletic performance call this "supercompensation," but most of us call it "getting better".

The trick is to figure out how long you should allow for recovery to get the best results. Just like everything else about running, the ideal amount of recovery time is different from person to person. And, of course, the harder the workout, the longer your recovery period should be.

If you're trying to train with maximum efficiency or you're just a masochist who likes to train as hard as you can as often as you can, you'll want to make your recovery periods as short as possible. Where some people might do a hard workout every two days, you might try reducing the recovery period to a day-and-a-half. Instead of Monday, Wednesday, and Friday mornings, maybe you'll try Monday morning, Tuesday night, Thursday morning, and Friday night, which lets you squeeze in an extra workout every week.

Most people should be more conservative than that to ensure they allow enough recovery time between hard workouts and don't overdo it. Maybe one fast workout and one long workout a week is enough for you to make progress while staying injury-free and allowing time for fun.

If I start to have too many days where it's hard to get out the door and run, that may be a sign that I've been overdoing it and need some extra rest. I'll schedule a few days of shorter runs or tell myself that I can cut my planned run short if I want. When I back off for a little while, my zest for running returns.

The great thing about allowing plenty of recovery time is that it allows you time to run with your friends, even those who aren't as fast as you are, and enjoy talking, running different routes, and running for its own sake.

Whatever your weekly routine, you'll also want to build larger cycles into your training routine. It's a good idea to routinely take a longer break than usual from your hard workouts to ensure that you get enough rest. My larger cycle consists of four weeks. For three weeks I do my regular series of workouts with the harder workouts mixed in. The fourth week is an easy week. My easy week has no speed work and no long runs. There's just some easy running that allows me to recover from the previous three weeks.

If you're running mostly for fun, and you like to race regularly, your training plan probably doesn't need to be any more complicated than that.

If you're trying to maximize your potential for a special

goal race you might want to organize your training in even larger cycles, a concept called "periodization". You could spend six months focused on building your endurance, a month building strength with extra hill running, a month focused on honing your speed, and then wrap it all up with a little extra rest just before the big race. Once you finish your target race, it's time to take a nice break to recover. Then you can get started on another cycle. You can run other races while you're training, but think of them as tempo runs or some other form of speed training when you include them in your schedule. Save your all-out effort for your goal race.

When setting up your training plan be careful about scheduling so much running that it takes away from your family or other important and fun activities. If you trade TV watching time for more time running, that's great. But if family, work, or weather get in the way of your plan, be flexible. One day here and there won't matter much in the long run. Adjust. Run at night instead of the morning if you have to. Or cut your run short. If you don't have time for the 10-mile run you planned, a 3-mile run is better than nothing.

Whatever you do, be realistic. Make sure your plan is achievable. As much as I would like to win every (who am I kidding, *any*) race I enter, I'm not that gifted. If I train with the goal of running a 2:10 marathon, I'll end up frustrated and injured.

Speaking of marathons, a lot of people who have been running a while and are ready for a new challenge think about giving the marathon a try. If you've been training regularly and you've done a number of races, you already have some idea how fast you are. Trying to finish a marathon sounds like a fun alternative. You'll need to run further, but that only requires doing more of what you already know you like to do.

Running a marathon is also good for your ego. Your

friends who don't run may not know that the marathon is a little over 26 miles long, but they do know that a marathon is something that those odd people who enjoy running think of as an important challenge. When you go out for a run in a snowstorm they may just think you're weird. But if you say you're running in the snow because you're training for a marathon, that impresses them. If they know you're a runner they've probably already asked if you've run a marathon, especially if you live in an area like Boston where the local race is a big event.

If your longest run is 10 miles once every week or two, you can find plenty of training plans that will set you up to run a marathon in four to six months. If everything goes well, you can sign up for the marathon, quickly ramp your long run up to 18 or 20 miles, and head to the start knowing that if you're determined you can finish the race.

But you will almost certainly suffer more than you have to. You're more likely to get hurt during training if you build up your mileage too fast, and if you don't run more than 20 miles (or do multiple 20-mile runs) in training the last few miles of your marathon will probably be hellish. I know this from experience. It's better to take a little more time and prepare thoroughly. There's always another race. I've said it before, but it's worth repeating. Your running will always be better in the long run if you're patient.

Training isn't just about building fitness. It's also about learning to run efficiently.

Nobody thinks they need to learn how to run. We've all been running since we were kids, using whatever style we picked up along the way. But if you try to run a marathon with the same form that you use for a mad dash around the bases in a softball game, you're going to work a lot harder than you have to, you're not going to be as fast as you could be, and sooner or later you're going to get hurt.

I have days when running is effortless. I just seem to flow along. I can increase my speed gracefully, without excessive pounding and flailing about. Running forever seems like an option. Those days are one of the main reasons that I'm addicted to running.

Unfortunately, those days are few and far between. But they're wonderful when they occur, so I keep fighting, through numerous runs full of effort and pain, trying to get that good feeling more often. I can compromise and minimize my suffering by running slowly, but that's not what I'm looking for.

I've been running for years, but my ability to find the most effective and comfortable running form still wavers from day to day. It's hard to keep everything operating properly all the time. There are a lot of things conspiring against me. My body, like most, has structural irregularities that I have to accommodate. Ice, snow, curbs, potholes, hills, rocks and roots, and the camber of the road all have an effect too. When I get tired my muscles don't always respond the way I want them to and it gets harder to stay focused.

To run well I need a body that's healthy and fit, but I also need the knowledge of what it means to run properly, the skill to apply that knowledge, and the focus to hold onto good running form once I find it. My goal is to ensure as much effort as possible is directed towards moving me forward while minimizing the pounding that occurs with each step and also minimizing anything that causes my head and torso to bounce up and down or twist excessively from side to side.

The most important thing I try to keep in mind in order to run efficiently is to keep my stride short and quick.

Try this for yourself. Stand up straight and start marching in place. Keep your lower legs, ankles, and feet relaxed.

Notice how the muscles in your abs, hips and quads work together to lift your knees. Notice how your hamstrings work to keep your lower legs from swinging out in front of you. Notice how your feet come off the ground heel-first. Notice how your feet land on the ball of your foot, then your ankle flexes until your heel reaches the ground and supports you.

Easy isn't it? There's hardly any stress at all when your foot hits the ground.

Now lean forward slightly. Don't bend at the waist, lean from your ankles so the rest of your body keeps its upright posture. Once you lean forward just a tiny bit, notice what happens. Your center of gravity moves ahead of your feet, you lose your balance, and gravity pulls you forward. When you start to fall forward, you automatically reach out with your leg and foot to brace yourself and keep from falling on your face. Your leg acts like a brake. You can feel that braking force jar your body as it stops your forward motion. Both of those, the jarring and the stopping, are bad things for a runner.

Start over. Stand up straight. Start marching in place, and lean forward again, just the tiniest bit. This time, step forward far enough to keep from falling, but not far enough to stop your forward motion. If you strike the right balance, you'll keep going forward with very little effort.

As you move forward keep your lower legs and feet soft and relaxed, just like you did when you were marching in place. Remember to lean from your ankles. Keep your lower back relaxed too. Use your abs to support and balance your upper body. Don't bend forward or back at the waist. If you do, your low back muscles need to do more of the work of holding you up and you're likely to end up with a backache.

That's what I try for when I'm running. If I do it right, each stride is short and quick. With each step I can feel the force from my legs pushing against the road traveling straight through my hips and the rest of my body, smoothly propelling me forward. When I want to go faster, I just lean forward a little more. My cadence, the number of strides per minute, remains about the same, but my stride lengthens a little (not too far though) and I go forward faster. Gravity does most of the work to pull me forward. All I have to do is keep from falling.

If I'm not running smoothly that usually means I'm reaching out too far forward with each step, or "overstriding". When I overstride I'm fighting gravity instead of letting it carry me ahead. My muscles, especially my shins and hamstrings, have to absorb extra pounding with every step and I have to expend more effort to keep running at the same pace.

When things start to go wrong my first reaction is to tighten up and try to fight through. That's exactly the wrong thing to do, but it's a hard habit to overcome. When I start to overstride I need to adjust my lean and shorten my stride until I get comfortable again. Once I'm able to relax, I usually end up going faster than when I was tense and trying too hard.

I don't need to worry about understriding. If my stride is too short, I have to keep increasing my cadence or I'm going to fall on my face. I can't keep that up for long, so understriding is self-correcting.

Going uphill I have to fight against gravity, so I'll shorten my stride a little more to keep my feet underneath me and ensure that each step pushes me forward and up. Leaning forward into the hill comes naturally. All I have to do is make sure I'm leaning from my ankles and not bending at the waist.

It's harder for me to maintain good form when I'm running downhill. The principle is the same – short strides, a slight forward lean, keep my lower legs relaxed, and let gravity do the work. Curling my upper body forward slightly can help keep me balanced. I'm fine until the hill gets just a little too steep. When that happens, I usually start going too fast. I can't move my legs fast enough to keep my balance, so I end up leaning back. My feet get out in front of me and I overstride to slow down and keep from falling. If I'm not in a hurry, I can slow down enough to minimize the pounding that follows, but if I'm in a race I have a bad habit of gritting my teeth and clomping down the hill. I get down the hill faster but my legs and back get beat up. That affects me for the rest of the race and often leaves me sore afterwards.

It's also hard to maintain my form when I'm tired. When I've been running for a long time and start to get weary I have a tendency to sit back on my heels and plod. The extra pounding from that makes me wear down even faster. If I keep it up my stride deteriorates into a survival shuffle. It takes a significant mental effort to focus on keeping good form when I'm tired, but if I'm successful I run better, and concentrating on my form also helps keep me from thinking about how tired and sore I am by the end of a long, hard run.

All this is a lot to keep in mind when you're running. Trying to get all of it right at once can be confusing. Sometimes it works and sometimes it's work. I still struggle with my form daily, but I keep plugging at it.

I can tell my form has improved because my shoes last longer than they used to. When my form started to get better I could run longer without the extra cushioning that I got from a new pair of shoes.

Overstriding is so common that most running shoes are designed with thicker cushioning in the heels to help protect runners who land on their heels. If you're not running properly that extra cushioning will help temporarily, but if you're racing or running long distances and you keep grinding along with poor form, sooner or later you will break down.

To check whether I'm landing on my heels I put a thin layer of Shoe Goo, a rubber adhesive, where the wear shows on the bottom edge of the heels of my shoes. If the Shoo Goo is still there after my run, I've done well.

There are shoes designed to help improve running form. Some of them have extra cushioning in the forefoot and less in the heel to help encourage runners to keep their weight forward. Other shoes try to mimic barefoot running. They provide very little cushioning while still furnishing some protection for a runner's feet. The idea is that if you run properly you won't need the cushioning. The downside is that you'd better run properly, or else.

I've tried those shoes, but I've found that I need some heel in my shoes. Shoes with lower heels put more stress on a runner's calf muscles and achilles tendons. My calves are not very flexible, so I use shoes with some lift in the heel to reduce the strain.

A metronome can help you learn to use to a shorter, quicker stride. I have a small clip-on metronome that's suitable for running and I have a metronome app for my iPod Touch. With a metronome to guide you, you don't have to think about your cadence as much and you can focus on the other elements of your form. For most people, a cadence of 85-to-90 steps per foot per minute is about right. I set my metronome to 180 beats per minute, so there's a beat for every step. If I set it at a lower rate so there's a beat every other step or every third step, I start to hammer out the beat with whichever foot happens to be landing at the time instead of running smoothly.

Everybody's body is different, so each person's correct running form is a little different from everyone else's. Read about "pose method running", "chi running", or the "Feldenkrais Method" for different discussions of efficient running form. Experiment with yourself. Try changing things a little bit, following the tips you've read or ones you get from a coach or another runner. See what works for you. It's worth the effort.

If you have the time to try other things, or if you start to get a little bored if you don't do anything other than running, try crosstraining. Adding other activities to your routine can be fun and help your running too. Exercising the muscles that running doesn't use helps maintain a balance that keeps you healthier and gives you a break from the pounding of your running workouts.

Almost any physical pastime can count as crosstraining. I do some biking, hiking, cross-country skiing, weight training, and kayaking. I know other runners who are into yoga, pilates, elliptical trainers, and swimming. That's just a start. Even work can count. If you move boxes, lay brick, or pitch hay, you're building strength that can help your running.

I never thought much about kayaking until I met Ruth, but I was surprised how much it helps with my running. It's especially good at helping to develop strength in my abs, and it helps with my cardiovascular conditioning too. Sitting in a kayak cockpit for long periods with my legs stretched out in front of me also serves as a good reminder to keep working on the flexibility of my hips and hamstrings.

Crosstraining isn't just about fitness. It can expand your social life. If you start working out with a skiing, swimming, or biking group you'll make a whole new set of friends.

When I'm injured I try to find a crosstraining activity that doesn't aggravate the injury. It takes the place of running temporarily to help me maintain my fitness until I'm ready to run again. It also helps to keep me from going mad from inactivity while I'm healing.

I do have to be careful when I jump into things I don't do regularly. For example, even if I haven't been skiing much, I'm fit enough from running to ski all afternoon but I'll be really sore afterwards.

One downside to crosstraining is that some things, like biking, kayaking or skiing, require a lot more gear. This adds to the appeal for some people but it can get expensive. When I met Ruth she got me into kayaking and cross-country skiing while I was getting her back into running. She only had to buy some shoes, but I had to get a boat and all the gear that goes with that, plus a ski package. But it was worth it.

Whatever training plan you choose, it takes pure faith to stick with the plan. It takes faith that your plan will prepare you to run fast enough or far enough to meet you goals. Then, when race day arrives, that faith helps keep negative thoughts out of your head so you can do what you've trained to do. Some people get the reassurance they need to be a successful runner by working with training plans they get from running experts, or by discussing their plans with more experienced friends. My greatest source for the necessary faith is my own experience from years of running. Other people taught me a lot, but I needed successes and failures of my own to learn what works for me.

Ray Charbonneau

About the Author

I live in Arlington Massachusetts with my wife, Ruth Sespaniak, and our two cats, Felix and Phoebe. Ruth and I can often be found running on the streets of Arlington, but Felix and Phoebe stay inside.

Running has touched my life in many ways, large and small. In 1999, I was searching for an Internet domain name to use for my personal web site and email. I wanted a name that was meaningful but most of the names I thought of were already taken so I needed something a little different. I was working in IT and the Y2K issue was big at the time. I took that and mixed it with the marathon distance (42 kilometers) to come up with "Y42K".

Since then, many people have asked me, "Y42K?" Some days "Y42K?" asks the question "Why run a marathon?" On better days, it asks "Why stop there?" It's also sort of Shakespearian-sounding, which adds a needed touch of gravitas.

As a result, you can see the odds and ends I post online at www.y42k.com, and if you have any comments on the book, good running stories, or know of a good way to dispose of used running shoes, you can contact me at writeray@y42k.com.

Made in the USA
Lexington, KY
20 October 2010